THE LITTLE BOOK BOOK

OF

VALUATION

Little Book Big Profits Series

In the *Little Book Big Profits* series, the brightest icons in the financial world write on topics that range from tried-and-true investment strategies to tomorrow's new trends. Each book offers a unique perspective on investing, allowing the reader to pick and choose from the very best in investment advice today.

Books in the *Little Book Big Profits* series include:

The Little Book That Still Beats the Market by Joel Greenblatt
The Little Book of Value Investing by Christopher Browne
The Little Book of Common Sense Investing by John C. Bogle
The Little Book That Makes You Rich by Louis Navellier
The Little Book That Builds Wealth by Pat Dorsey
The Little Book That Saves Your Assets by David M. Darst
The Little Book of Bull Moves by Peter D. Schiff
The Little Book of Main Street Money by Jonathan Clements
The Little Book of Safe Money by Jason Zweig
The Little Book of Behavioral Investing by James Montier
The Little Book of Big Dividends by Charles B. Carlson
The Little Book of Bulletproof Investing by Ben Stein and Phil DeMuth
The Little Book of Commodity Investing by John R. Stephenson
The Little Book of Economics by Greg Ip
The Little Book of Sideways Markets by Vitaliy N. Katsenelson
The Little Book of Currency Trading by Kathy Lien
The Little Book of Alternative Investments by Ben Stein and Phil DeMuth
The Little Book of Valuation by Aswath Damodaran

THE LITTLE BOOK

OF

VALUATION

How to Value a Company,

Pick a Stock, and Profit

ASWATH DAMODARAN

WILEY

John Wiley & Sons, Inc.

Published by John Wiley & Sons, Inc., Hoboken, New Jersey.
Published simultaneously in Canada.

For general information on our other products and services or for technical support, please contact our Customer Care Department within the United States at (800) 762-2974, outside the United States at (317) 572-3993 or fax (317) 572-4002.

Wiley also publishes its books in a variety of electronic formats. Some content that appears in print may not be available in electronic books. For more information about Wiley products, visit our web site at www.wiley.com.

Library of Congress Cataloging-in-Publication Data:
Damodaran, Aswath.
    The little book of valuation : how to value a company, pick a stock and profit / Aswath Damodaran.
        p. cm. — (Little book big profit)
    ISBN 978-1-118-00477-7 (cloth); 978-1-118-06412-2 (ebk); 978-1-118-06413-9 (ebk);
        978-1-118-06414-6 (ebk)
    1. Corporations—Valuation.   2. Stocks—Prices.   3. Investment analysis.   I. Title.
HG4028.V3D3535 2011
332.63'221—dc22

                                                                                    2010053543

Printed in the United States of America
10   9   8   7   6   5   4   3   2   1

To all of those who have been subjected to my long discourses on valuation, this is my penance.

Contents

Hit the Ground Running—
Valuation Basics

Foreword

IF YOU TAKE A MOMENT TO THINK ABOUT IT, stock exchanges provide a service that seems miraculous. They allow you to exchange cash that you don't need today for a share in a claim, based on the future cash flows of a company, which should grow in value over time. You can defer consumption now in order to consume more in the future. The process also goes in reverse. You can sell shares in a company for cash, effectively trading tomorrow's potential for a certain sum today. Valuation is the mechanism behind this wondrous ability to trade cash for claims. And if you want to invest thoughtfully, you must learn how to value.

As a student and practitioner of valuation techniques throughout my career, I can say without hesitation that Aswath Damodaran is the best teacher of valuation I have ever encountered. I have attended his lectures, consulted his books, pored over his papers, and scoured his web site. He combines remarkable breadth and depth with clarity and practicality. He intimately knows valuation's big ideas as well as its nooks and crannies, and delivers the content in a useful and sensible way. If you are looking to learn about valuation from the master, you have come to the right place.

The Little Book of Valuation may not be large, but it packs a lot of punch. You'll start off learning about the basics of discounted cash flow and quickly move to valuation multiples. Professor Damodaran also frames a proper mind-set—valuations are biased and wrong, and simpler can be better—and emphasizes the difference between intrinsic and relative approaches. His discussion of the pros and cons of popular valuation multiples is especially useful.

Valuing businesses at different stages of their lives is tricky. For example, how do you compare the relative attractiveness of a hot initial public offering of a company boasting the latest whiz-bang technology to a stable but staid manufacturer of consumer products? In the heart of the book, Professor Damodaran helps you navigate the valuation issues that surround companies at different points in their life cycles, providing vivid and relevant examples that help cement the ideas.

The book's final section guides you in dealing with some of the special situations that you are likely to encounter. For instance, valuing a company that relies on a commodity that rises and falls like a roller coaster is an inherently thorny problem. So, too, is valuing a company that pours money into research and development with little that is tangible to show for it. These are some of the valuation challenges you will face as a practitioner, but are also among the most rewarding.

Don't put the book down until you have read, and internalized, the "10 Rules for the Road" in the conclusion. They effectively meld good theory and practice, and will guide you when you reach a point of uncertainty.

Valuation is at the core of the economic activity in a free economy. As a consequence, a working knowledge of valuation's broad concepts as well as its ins and outs is of great utility. Aswath Damodaran has done more to bring these ideas to life than anyone I know. I hope that you enjoy *The Little Book of Valuation* and profit from its lessons.

Michael J. Mauboussin

Michael J. Mauboussin is chief investment strategist at Legg Mason Capital Management and an adjunct professor at Columbia Business School.

Introduction

————— ❧ —————

DO YOU KNOW WHAT A SHARE IN GOOGLE OR APPLE is really worth? What about that condo or house you just bought? Should you care? Knowing the value of a stock, bond, or property may not be a prerequisite for successful investing, but it does help you make more informed judgments.

Most investors see valuing an asset as a daunting task—something far too complex and complicated for their skill sets. Consequently, they leave it to the professionals (equity research analysts, appraisers) or ignore it entirely. I believe that valuation, at its core, is simple, and anyone who is willing to spend time collecting and analyzing information can do it. I show you how in this book.

I also hope to strip away the mystique from valuation practices and provide ways in which you can look at valuation judgments made by analysts and appraisers and decide for yourself whether they make sense or not.

While valuation models can be filled with details, the value of any company rests on a few key drivers, which will vary from company to company. In the search for these *value drivers*, I will look not only across the life cycle from young growth firms such as Under Armour to mature companies like Hormel Foods, but also across diverse sectors from commodity companies such as Exxon Mobil, to financial service companies such as Wells Fargo, and pharmaceutical companies such as Amgen.

Here is the bonus: If you understand the value drivers of a business, you can also start to identify *value plays*—stocks that are investment bargains. By the end of the book, I would like you to be able to assess the value of any company or business that you are interested in buying and use this understanding to become a more informed and successful investor.

Not all of you will have the time or the inclination to value companies. But this book will give you the tools if you choose to try, and it will provide you with some shortcuts in case you do not.

Let's hit the road.

In a web site to accompany this book (www.wiley .com/go/littlebookofvaluation), you can look at these valuation models and change or update the numbers to see the effects.

THE LITTLE BOOK

OF
VALUATION

Hit the Ground Running—
Valuation Basics

Chapter One

Value—More Than a Number!

Understanding the Terrain

OSCAR WILDE DEFINED A CYNIC AS ONE WHO "knows the price of everything and the value of nothing." The same can be said of many investors who regard investing as a game and define winning as staying ahead of the pack.

A postulate of sound investing is that an investor does not pay more for an asset than it is worth. If you accept this proposition, it follows that you have to at least try to value whatever you are buying before buying it. I know there are those who argue that value is in the eyes of the beholder, and that any price can be justified if there are other investors who perceive an investment to be worth that amount. That is patently absurd. Perceptions may be all that matter when the asset is a painting or a sculpture, but you buy financial assets for the cash flows that you expect to receive. The price of a stock cannot be justified by merely using the argument that there will be other investors around who will pay a higher price in the future. That is the equivalent of playing an expensive game of musical chairs, and the question becomes: Where will you be when the music stops?

Two Approaches to Valuation

Ultimately, there are dozens of valuation models but only two valuation approaches: *intrinsic* and *relative*. In intrinsic valuation, we begin with a simple proposition: The intrinsic value of an asset is determined by the cash flows you expect that asset to generate over its life and how uncertain you feel about these cash flows. Assets with high and stable cash flows should be worth more than assets with low and volatile cash flows. You should pay more for a property that has long-term renters paying a high rent than for a more speculative property with not only lower rental income, but more variable vacancy rates from period to period.

While the focus in principle should be on intrinsic valuation, most assets are valued on a relative basis. In relative valuation, assets are valued by looking at how the market prices similar assets. Thus, when determining what to pay for a house, you would look at what similar houses in the neighborhood sold for. With a stock, that means comparing its pricing to similar stocks, usually in its "peer group." Thus, Exxon Mobil will be viewed as a stock to buy if it is trading at 8 times earnings while other oil companies trade at 12 times earnings.

While there are purists in each camp who argue that the other approach is useless, there is a middle ground. Intrinsic valuation provides a fuller picture of what drives the value of a business or stock, but there are times when relative valuation will yield a more realistic estimate of value. In general, there is no reason to choose one over the other, since nothing stops you from using both approaches on the same investment. In truth, you can improve your odds by investing in stocks that are undervalued not only on an intrinsic basis but also on a relative one.

Why Should You Care?

Investors come to the market with a wide range of investment philosophies. Some are market timers looking to buy before market upturns, while others believe in picking stocks based on growth and future earnings potential.

Some pore over price charts and classify themselves as technicians, whereas others compute financial ratios and swear by fundamental analysis, in which they drill down on the specific cash flows that a company can generate and derive a value based on these cash flows. Some invest for short-term profits and others for long-term gains. Knowing how to value assets is useful to all of these investors, though its place in the process will vary. Market timers can use valuation tools at the start of the process to determine whether a group or class of assets (stocks, bonds, or real estate) is under- or overvalued, while stock pickers can draw on valuations of individual companies to decide which stocks are cheap and which ones are expensive. Even technical analysts can use valuations to detect shifts in momentum, when a stock on an upward path changes course and starts going down or vice versa.

Increasingly, though, the need to assess value has moved beyond investments and portfolio management. There is a role for valuation at every stage of a firm's life cycle. For small private businesses thinking about expanding, valuation plays a key role when they approach venture capital and private equity investors for more capital. The share of a firm that venture capitalists will demand in exchange for a capital infusion will depend upon the value they estimate for the firm. As the companies get larger and decide to go public, valuations determine the prices at which they are offered to the market in the public offering. Once established, decisions on where to invest, how much to borrow, and how much to return to the owners will all be decisions that are affected by perceptions of their impact on value. Even accounting is not immune. The most significant global trend in accounting standards is a shift toward fair value accounting, where assets are valued on balance sheets at their fair values rather than at their original cost. Thus, even a casual perusal of financial statements requires an understanding of valuation fundamentals.

Some Truths about Valuation

Before delving into the details of valuation, it is worth noting some general truths about valuation that will provide you not only with perspective when looking at valuations done by others, but also with some comfort when doing your own.

All Valuations Are Biased

You almost never start valuing a company or stock with a blank slate. All too often, your views on a company or stock are formed before you start inputting the numbers into the models and metrics that you use and, not surprisingly, your conclusions tend to reflect your biases.

The bias in the process starts with the companies you choose to value. These choices are not random. It may be that you have read something in the press (good or bad) about the company or heard from a talking head that a particular company was under- or overvalued. It continues when you collect the information you need to value the firm. The annual report and other financial statements include not only the accounting numbers but also management discussions of performance, often putting the best possible spin on the numbers.

With professional analysts, there are *institutional factors* that add to this already substantial bias. Equity research analysts, for instance, issue more buy than sell recommendations because they need to maintain good relations with the companies they follow and also because of the pressures that they face from their own employers, who generate other business from these companies. To these institutional factors, add the *reward and punishment structure* associated with finding companies to be under- and overvalued. Analysts whose compensation is dependent upon whether they find a firm to be cheap or expensive will be biased in that direction.

The inputs that you use in the valuation will reflect your optimistic or pessimistic bent; thus, you are more likely to use higher growth rates and see less risk in companies that you are predisposed to like. There is also *post-valuation garnishing*, where you increase your estimated value by adding premiums for the good stuff (synergy, control, and management quality) or reduce your estimated value by netting out discounts for the bad stuff (illiquidity and risk).

Always be honest about your biases: Why did you pick this company to value? Do you like or dislike the company's management? Do you already own stock in the company? Put these biases down on paper, if possible, before you start. In addition, confine your background research on the company to information sources rather than opinion sources; in other words, spend more time looking at a company's financial statements than reading equity research reports about the company. If you are looking at someone else's valuation of a company, always consider the reasons for the valuation and the potential biases that may affect the analyst's judgments. As a general rule, the more bias there is in the process, the less weight you should attach to the valuation judgment.

Most Valuations (even good ones) Are Wrong

Starting early in life, you are taught that if you follow the right steps, you will get the correct answer, and that if the answer is imprecise, you must have done something wrong. While precision is a good measure of process in mathematics or physics, it is a poor measure of quality in valuation. Your best estimates for the future will not match up to the actual numbers for several reasons. First, even if your information sources are impeccable, you have to convert raw information into forecasts, and any mistakes that you make at this stage will cause *estimation error*. Next, the path that you envision for a firm can prove to be hopelessly off. The firm may do much better or much worse than you expected it to perform, and the resulting earnings and cash flows will be different from your estimates; consider this *firm-specific uncertainty*. When valuing Cisco in 2001, for instance, I seriously underestimated how difficult it would be for the company to maintain its acquisition-driven growth in the future, and I overvalued the company as a consequence. Finally, even if a firm evolves exactly the way you expected it to, the macro-economic environment can change in unpredictable ways. Interest rates can go up or down and the economy can do much better or worse than expected. My valuation of Goldman Sachs from August 2008 looks hopelessly optimistic, in hindsight, because I did not foresee the damage wrought by the banking crisis of 2008.

The amount and type of uncertainty you face can vary across companies, with consequences for investors. One implication is that you cannot judge a valuation by its precision, since you will face more uncertainty when you value a young growth company than when you value a mature company. Another is that avoiding dealing with uncertainty will not make it go away. Refusing to value a business because you are too uncertain about its future prospects makes no sense, since everyone else looking at the business faces the same uncertainty. Finally, collecting more information and doing more analysis will not necessarily translate into less uncertainty. In some cases, ironically, it can generate more uncertainty.

Simpler Can Be Better

Valuations have become more and more complex over the last two decades, as a consequence of two developments. On the one side, computers and calculators are more powerful and accessible than they used to be, making it easier to analyze data. On the other side, information is both more plentiful and easier to access and use.

A fundamental question in valuation is how much detail to bring into the process, and the trade-off is straightforward. More detail gives you a chance to use specific information to make better forecasts, but it also creates the need for more inputs, with the potential for error on each one, and it generates more complicated and opaque models. Drawing from the principle of parsimony, common in the physical sciences, here is a simple rule: When valuing an asset, use the simplest model that you can. If you can value an asset with three inputs, don't use five. If you can value a company with three years of forecasts, forecasting 10 years of cash flows is asking for trouble. Less is more.

Start Your Engines!

Most investors choose not to value companies and offer a variety of excuses: valuation models are too complex, there is insufficient information, or there is too much uncertainty. While all of these reasons have a kernel of truth to them, there is no reason why they should stop you from trying. Valuation models can be simplified and you can make do with the information you have and—yes—the future will always be uncertain. Will you be wrong sometimes? Of course, but so will everyone else. Success in investing comes not from being right but from being wrong less often than everyone else.

Power Tools
of the Trade

Time Value, Risk, and Statistics

SHOULD YOU BUY GOOGLE (GOOG), a company that pays no dividends now but has great growth potential and lots of uncertainty about its future, or Altria (MO), a high dividend-paying company with limited growth prospects and stable income? Is Altria cheap, relative to other tobacco companies? To make these assessments, you have to compare cash flows today to cash flows in the future, to evaluate how risk affects value, and be able to deal with a large amount of information. The tools to do so are provided in this chapter.

Time Is Money

The simplest tools in finance are often the most powerful. The notion that a dollar today is preferable to a dollar in the future is intuitive enough for most people to grasp without the use of models and mathematics. The principles of *present value* enable us to calculate exactly how much a dollar sometime in the future is worth in today's terms, and to compare cash flows across time.

There are three reasons why a cash flow in the future is worth less than a similar cash flow today.

1. People prefer consuming today to consuming in the future.
2. Inflation decreases the purchasing power of cash over time. A dollar in the future will buy less than a dollar would today.
3. A promised cash flow in the future may not be delivered. There is risk in waiting.

The process by which future cash flows are adjusted to reflect these factors is called discounting, and the magnitude of these factors is reflected in the *discount rate*. The discount rate can be viewed as a composite of the expected *real return* (reflecting consumption preferences), expected inflation (to capture the purchasing power of the cash flow), and a premium for uncertainty associated with the cash flow.

The process of discounting converts future cash flows into cash flows in today's terms. There are five types of cash flows—simple cash flows, annuities, growing annuities, perpetuities, and growing perpetuities.

A *simple cash flow* is a single cash flow in a specified future time period. Discounting a cash flow converts it into today's dollars (or present value) and enables the user to compare cash flows at different points in time. The present value of a cash flow is calculated thus:

$$\frac{\text{Cash flow in future period}}{(1 + \text{Disount rate})^{\text{Time period}}}$$

Thus, the present value of $1,000 in 10 years, with a discount rate of 8 percent, is:

$$\frac{1000}{(1.08)^{10}} = \$463.19$$

Other things remaining equal, the value of a dollar in the future will decrease the further into the future it is, and the more uncertain you feel about getting it.

An *annuity* is a constant cash flow that occurs at regular intervals for a fixed period of time. While you can compute the present value by discounting each cash flow and adding up the numbers, you can also use this equation:

$$\text{Annual cash flow} \left[\frac{1 - \dfrac{1}{(1 + \text{Discount rate})^{\text{Number of periods}}}}{\text{Discount rate}} \right]$$

To illustrate, assume again that you have a choice of buying a car for $10,000 cash down or paying installments of $3,000 a year, at the end of each year, for five years, for the same car. If the discount rate is 12 percent, the present value of the installment plan is:

$$\$3,000 \left[\frac{1 - \dfrac{1}{(1.12)^5}}{.12} \right] = \$10,814$$

The cash-down plan costs less, in present value terms, than the installment plan.

A *growing annuity* is a cash flow that grows at a constant rate for a specified period of time. Suppose you have the rights to a gold mine that generated $1.5 million in cash flows last year and is expected to continue to generate cash flows for the next 20 years. If you assume a growth rate of 3 percent a year in the cash flows and a discount rate of 10 percent to reflect your uncertainty about these cash flows, the present value of the gold from this mine is $16.146 million;* this value will increase as the growth rate increases and will decrease as the discount rate rises.

A *perpetuity* is a constant cash flow at regular intervals *forever* and the present value is obtained by dividing the cash flow by the discount rate. The most common example offered for a perpetuity is a *console bond*, a bond that pays a fixed interest payment (or coupon) forever.

*There is a present value equation that exists for this computation:

$$= \text{Cash flow}(1+g) \left[\frac{1 - \dfrac{(1+g)^n}{(1+r)^n}}{(r-g)} \right] = 1.5(1.03) \left[\frac{1 - \dfrac{1.03^{20}}{1.10^{20}}}{(.10 - .03)} \right] = 16.146$$

You can also arrive at the same number by computing the present value of each cash flow and adding up the numbers.

The value of a console bond that pays a $60 coupon each year, if the interest rate is 9 percent, is as follows:

$$\$60/0.09 = \$667$$

A *growing perpetuity* is a cash flow that is expected to grow at a constant rate forever. The present value of a growing perpetuity can be written as:

$$\frac{\text{Expected cash flow next year}}{(\text{Discount rate} - \text{Expected growth rate})}$$

Although a growing perpetuity and a growing annuity share several features, the fact that a growing perpetuity lasts forever puts constraints on the growth rate. The growth rate has to be less than the discount rate for the equation to work, but an even tighter constraint is that the growth rate used has to be lower than the nominal growth rate of the economy, since no asset can have cash flows growing faster than that rate forever.

Consider a simple example. Assume that you are assessing a stock that paid $2 as dividends last year. Assume that you expect these dividends to grow 2 percent a year in perpetuity, and that your required rate of return for investing in this stock, given its risk, is 8 percent.

With these inputs, you can value the stock using a perpetual growth model:

$$\frac{\text{Expected dividends next year}}{(\text{Required return} - \text{Expected growth rate})} = \frac{\$2\,(1.02)}{(.08 - .02)} = \$34.00$$

These cash flows are the essential building blocks for virtual every financial asset. Bonds, stocks, or real estate properties can ultimately be broken down into sets of cash flows. If you can discount these cash flows, you can value all of these assets.

Grappling with Risk

When stocks were first traded in the sixteen and seventeenth centuries, there was little access to information and few ways of processing that limited information. Only the very wealthy invested in stocks, and even they were susceptible to scams. As new investors entered the financial markets at the start of the twentieth century, services started to collect return and price data on individual securities and to compute basic measures of risk, though these measures remained for the most part simplistic. For instance, a railroad stock that paid a large dividend was considered less risky than stock in a manufacturing or shipping venture.

In the early 1950s, a doctoral student at the University of Chicago named Harry Markowitz noted that the risk of a portfolio could be written as a function not only of how much was invested in each security and the risks of the individual securities, but also of how these securities moved together. If securities that move in different directions are in the same portfolio, he noted that the risk of the portfolio could be lower than the risk of individual securities, and that investors should get a much better trade-off from taking risk by holding diversified portfolios than by holding individual stocks.

To illustrate this, consider the risks you are exposed to when you invest in a company such as Disney (DIS). Some of the risks you face are specific to the company: Its next animated movie may do better than expected and its newest theme park in Hong Kong may draw fewer visitors than projected. Some of the risks affect not just Disney but its competitors in the business: Legislation that changes the nature of the television business can alter the profitability of Disney's ABC network, and the ratings at the network will be determined by the strength of its new shows relative to competitors. Still other risks come from macroeconomic factors and affect most or all companies in the market to varying degrees: Rising interest rates or an economic recession will put a dent in the profitability of all companies. Take note that you can get better or worse news than expected on each of these dimensions. If you invest all your money in Disney, you are exposed to all of these risks. If you own Disney as part of a larger portfolio of many stocks, the risks that affect one or a few firms will get averaged out in your portfolio: For every company where something worse than expected happens, there will be another company where something better than expected will happen. The macroeconomic risk that affects many or most firms cannot be diversified away. In the Markowitz world, this *market risk* is the only risk that you should consider, as an investor in a publicly traded company.

If you accept the Markowitz proposition that the only risk you care about is the risk that you cannot diversify away, how do you measure the exposure of a company to this market-wide risk? The most widely used model is the capital asset pricing model, or the CAPM, developed in the early 1960s. In this model, you assume that investors face no transaction costs and share the same information. Since there is no cost to diversifying and no gain from not doing so, each investor holds a supremely diversified portfolio composed of all traded assets (called the *market portfolio*). The risk of any asset then becomes the risk added to this "market portfolio," which is measured with a *beta*. The beta is a relative risk measure and it is standardized around one; a stock with a beta above one is more exposed to market risk than the average stock, and a stock with a beta below one is less exposed. The *expected return* on the investment can then be written as:

Risk-free rate + Beta (Risk premium for average risk investment)

The CAPM is intuitive and simple to use, but it is based on unrealistic assumptions. To add to the disquiet, studies over the last few decades suggest that CAPM betas do not do a very good job in explaining differences in returns across stocks. Consequently, two classes of models have developed as alternatives to the CAPM. The first are multi-beta models, which measure the risk added by an investment to a diversified portfolio, with many betas (rather than the single beta), and with each beta measuring exposure to a different type of market risk (with its own risk premium). The second are proxy models, which look at the characteristics (such as small market capitalization and price-to-book ratio) of companies that have earned high returns in the past and use those as measures of risk.

It is indisputable that all these models are flawed, either because they make unrealistic assumptions or because the parameters cannot be estimated precisely. However, there is no disputing that:

- *Risk matters.* Even if you don't agree with portfolio theory, you cannot ignore risk while investing.
- *Some investments are riskier than others.* If you don't use beta as a measure of relative risk, you have to come up with an alternative measure of relative risk.
- *The price of risk affects value, and markets set this price.*

You may not buy into the CAPM or multi-beta models, but you have to devise ways of measuring and incorporating risk into your investment decisions.

Accounting 101

There are three basic accounting statements. The first is the *balance sheet*, which summarizes the assets owned by a firm, the value of these assets, and the mix of debt and equity used to fund them, at a point in time. The *income statement* provides information on the operations of the firm and its profitability over time. The *statement of cash flows* specifies how much cash the firm generated or spent from its operating, financing, and investing activities.

How do accountants measure the value of assets? For most *fixed and long-term assets*, such as land, buildings, and equipment, they begin with what you originally paid for the asset (historical cost) and reduce that value for the aging of the asset (depreciation or amortization). For *short-term assets* (current assets), including inventory (raw materials, works in progress, and finished goods), receivables (summarizing moneys owed to the firm), and cash, accountants are more amenable to the use of an updated or market value. If a company invests in the securities or assets of another company, the investment is valued at an updated market value if the investment is held for trading and historical cost when it is not. In the special case where the holding comprises more than 50 percent of the value of another company (subsidiary), the firm has to record all of the subsidiary's assets and liabilities on its balance sheet (this is called *consolidation*), with a *minority interest* item capturing the percentage of the subsidiary that does not belong to it. Finally, you have what are loosely categorized as *intangible assets*. While you would normally consider items such as brand names, customer loyalty, and a well-trained work force as intangible assets, the most commonly encountered intangible asset in accounting is goodwill. When a firm acquires another firm, the price it pays is first allocated to the existing assets of the acquired firm. Any excess paid becomes goodwill and is recorded as an asset. If the accountants determine that the value of the target company has dropped since the acquisition, this goodwill has to be decreased or impaired.

Just as with the measurement of asset value, the accounting categorization of liabilities and equity is governed by a set of fairly rigid principles. *Current liabilities* include obligations that the firm has coming due in the next accounting period, such as accounts payable and short-term borrowing, and these items are usually recorded at their current market value. *Long-term debt*, including bank loans and corporate bonds, are generally recorded at the face value at the time of issue and are generally not marked-to-market. Finally, the accounting measure of equity shown on the balance sheet reflects the original proceeds received by the firm when it issued the equity, augmented by any earnings made since then (or reduced by losses, if any) and reduced by any dividends paid out and stock buybacks.

Two principles underlie the measurement of accounting earnings and profitability. The first is accrual accounting, where the revenue from selling a good or service is recognized in the period in which the good is sold or the service is performed (in whole or substantially), and a corresponding effort is made to match expenses incurred to generate revenues. The second is the categorization of expenses into operating, financing, and capital expenses. Operating expenses are expenses that at least in theory provide benefits only for the current period; the cost of labor and materials expended to create products that are sold in the current period is a good example. Financing expenses are expenses arising from the non-equity financing used to raise capital for the business; the most common example is interest expenses. Capital expenses are expected to generate benefits over multiple periods; for instance, the cost of buying machinery and buildings is treated as a capital expense, and is spread over time as depreciation or amortization. Netting operating expenses and depreciation from revenues yields *operating income*, whereas the income after interest and taxes is termed *net income*.

To measure profitability on a relative basis, you can scale profits to revenues to estimate *margins*, both from an operating standpoint (*operating margin* = operating income/sales) and to equity investors (*net margin* = net income/sales). To measure how well a firm is investing its capital, we can look at the after-tax operating income relative to the *capital invested in the firm*, where capital is defined as the sum of the book values (BV) of debt and equity, net of cash, and marketable securities. This is the *return on capital* (ROC) or *return on invested capital* (ROIC) and it is computed as follows:

$$\text{After-tax ROC} = \frac{\text{Operating income}(1 - \text{tax rate})}{\text{BV of debt} + \text{BV of equity} - \text{Cash}}$$

The return on capital varies widely across firms in different businesses, tending to be lower in competitive businesses. The *return on equity* (ROE) examines profitability from the perspective of the equity investors by relating profits to the equity investor (net profit after taxes and interest expenses) to the book value of the equity investment and can be computed as:

$$\text{ROE} = \frac{\text{Net income}}{\text{Book value of common equity}}$$

An accounting balance sheet is useful because it provides us with information about a firm's history of investing and raising capital, but it is backward looking. To provide a more forward-looking picture, consider an alternative, the financial balance sheet, as illustrated in Table 2.1.

Table 2.1   A Financial Balance Sheet

	Measure	Explanation
	Assets in place	Value of investments already made, updated to reflect their current cash flow potential.
+	Growth assets	Value of investments the company is expected to make in the future (this rests on perceptions of growth opportunities).
=	Value of business	The value of a business is the sum of assets in place and growth assets.
−	Debt	Lenders get first claim on cash flows, during operations, and cash proceeds, in liquidation.
=	Value of equity	Equity investors get whatever is left over after debt payments.

While a financial balance sheet bears a superficial resemblance to the accounting balance sheet, it differs on two important counts. First, rather than classify assets based on asset life or tangibility, it categorizes them into investments already made by the company (assets in place) and investments that you expect the company to make in the future (growth assets). The second is that the values reflect not what has already been invested in these assets, but their current values, based upon expectations for the future. Since the assets are recorded at current value, the debt and equity values are also updated. Both U.S. and international accounting standards are pushing towards "fair value" accounting. Put simply, this would lead to accounting balance sheets more closely resembling financial balance sheets.

Making Sense of Data

The problem that we face in financial analysis today is not that we have too little information but that we have too much. Making sense of large and often contradictory information is part of analyzing companies. Statistics can make this job easier.

There are three ways to present data. The first and simplest is to provide the individual data items and let the user make sense of the data. Thus, an analyst, who compares the price earnings (PE) ratio for a chemical company with the PE ratios of four similar chemical companies is using individual data. As the number of data items mounts, it becomes more difficult to keep track of individual data and we look at ways to summarize the data. The most common of these summary statistics is the *average* across all data items, and the *standard deviation*, which measures the spread or deviation around the average. While summary statistics are useful, they can sometimes be misleading. Consequently, when presented with thousands of pieces of information, you can break the numbers down into individual values (or ranges of values) and indicate the number of individual data items that take on each value or range of values. This is called a *frequency distribution*. The advantages of presenting the data in a distribution are twofold. First, you can summarize even the largest data set into a distribution and get a measure of what values occur most frequently and the range of high and low values. The second is that the resulting distribution can resemble one of the many common statistical distributions. The normal distribution, for instance, is a symmetric distribution, with a peak centered in the middle of the distribution, and tails that stretch to include infinite positive or negative values. Not all distributions are symmetric, though. Some are weighted towards extreme positive values and are positively skewed, and some towards extreme negative values and are negatively skewed, as indicated in Figure 2.1.

Figure 2.1   Normal and Skewed Distributions

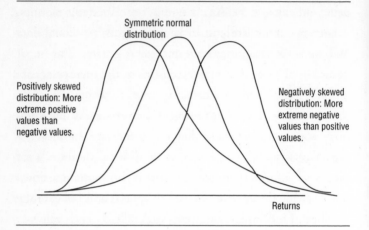

Why should you care? With skewed distributions, the average may not be a good measure of what is typical. It will be pushed up (down) by the extreme positive (negative) values in a positively (negatively) skewed distribution. With these distributions, it is the *median*, the midpoint of the distribution (with half of all data points being higher and half being lower), which is the better indicator.

When looking at two series of data it is useful to know whether and how movements in one variable affect the other. Consider, for instance, two widely followed variables, inflation and interest rates, and assume that you want to analyze how they move together. The simplest measure of this co-movement is the *correlation*. If interest rates go up, when inflation increases, the variables move together and have a positive correlation; if interest rates go down, when inflation increases, they have a negative correlation. A correlation close to zero indicates that interest rates and inflation have no relationship to each other. While a correlation tells you how two variables move together, a *simple regression* allows you to go further. Assume, for instance, that you wanted to examine how changes in inflation affect changes in interest rates. You would start by plotting 10 years of data on interest rates against inflation in a *scatterplot*, as shown in Figure 2.2.

Figure 2.2   Scatterplot of Interest Rates against Inflation

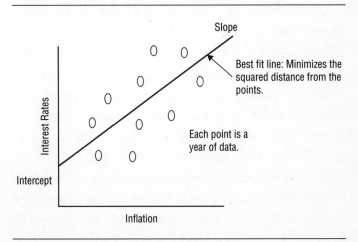

Each of the 10 points on the scatterplot represents a year of data. When the regression line is fit, two parameters emerge—one is the intercept of the regression, and the other is the slope of the regression line. Assume, in this case, that the regression output is as follows:

Interest rate = 1.5% + 0.8 (Inflation rate) R Squared = 60%

The *intercept* measures the value that interest rates will have when the inflation is zero; in this case, that value is 1.5 percent. The *slope (b)* of the regression measures how much interest rates will change for every 1 percent change in inflation; in this case that value is 0.8 percent. When the two variables are positively (negatively) correlated, the slope will also be positive (negative). The regression equation can be used to estimate predicted values for the dependent variable. Thus, if you expect inflation to be 2 percent, the interest rate will be 3.3 percent (1.5% + 0.8 * 2% = 3.3%). In a multiple regression, you extend this approach to try to explain a dependent variable with several independent variables. You could, for instance, attempt to explain changes in interest rates using both inflation and overall economic growth. With both simple and multiple regressions, the R-squared explains the percentage of the variation in the dependent variables that is explained by the independent variable or variables; thus, 60 percent of the variation in interest rates can be explained by changes in inflation.

The Tool Box Is Full

You can get a lot done with the tools developed in this chapter. Time value concepts can be used to compare and aggregate cash flows across time on investments. Risk and return models in finance allow us to derive costs of investing in companies, and by extension, to value companies in different businesses. Much of the earnings and cash flow data come from financial statements. Finally, given the sheer quantity of information that we have to access, statistical measures that compress the data and provide a sense of the relationships between data items can provide invaluable insight. Let us take this valuation tool box and go to work on specific companies.

Chapter Three

Yes, Virginia, Every Asset Has an Intrinsic Value

~

Determining Intrinsic Value

IMAGINE YOU ARE AN INVESTOR LOOKING to invest in a share of 3M (MMM), a firm that delivers a wide range of products that cater to the office and business market. Based upon the information that you have on the company right now, you could estimate the expected cash flows you would get from this investment and assess the risk in those cash flows. Converting these expectations into an estimate of the value of 3M is the focus of this chapter.

Value the Business or Just the Equity?

In discounted cash flow valuation, you discount expected cash flows back at a risk-adjusted rate. When applied in the context of valuing a company, one approach is to value the entire business, with both existing investments and growth assets; this is often termed *firm or enterprise valuation*. The other approach is to focus on valuing just the equity in the business. Table 3.1 frames the two approaches in terms of the financial balance items introduced in Chapter 2.

Table 3.1   Valuation Choices

	Measure	Explanation
	Assets in place	
+	Growth assets	
=	Value of business	To value the entire business, discount the cash flows before debt payments (cash flow to the firm) by overall cost of financing, including both debt and equity (cost of capital).
−	Debt	From the value of the business, subtract out debt to get to equity.
=	Value of equity	To value equity directly, discount the cash flows left over after debt payments (cash flows to equity) at the cost of equity.

Put in the context of the question of whether you should buy shares in 3M, here are your choices. You can value 3M as a business and subtract out the debt the company owes to get to the value of its shares. Or, you can value the equity in the company directly, by focusing on the cash flows 3M has left over after debt payments and adjusting for the risk in the stock. Done right, both approaches should yield similar estimates of value per share.

Inputs to Intrinsic Valuation

There are four basic inputs that we need for a value estimate: cash flows from existing assets (net of reinvestment needs and taxes); expected growth in these cash flows for a forecast period; the cost of financing the assets; and an estimate of what the firm will be worth at the end of the forecast period. Each of these inputs can be defined either from the perspective of the firm or just from the perspective of the equity investors. We will use 3M to illustrate each measure, using information from September 2008.

Cash Flows

The simplest and most direct measure of the cash flow you get from the company for buying its shares is dividends paid; 3M paid $1.38 billion in dividends in 2007.

One limitation of focusing on dividends is that many companies have shifted from dividends to stock buybacks as their mechanism for returning cash to stockholders. One simple way of adjusting for this is to *augment the dividend* with stock buybacks and look at the cumulative cash returned to stockholders.

Augmented dividends = Dividends + Stock buybacks

Unlike dividends, stock buybacks can spike in some years and may need to be averaged across a few years to arrive at more reasonable annualized numbers. In 2007, 3M bought back $3.24 billion in stock; adding this amount to the dividend of $1.38 billion results in augmented dividends of $4.62 billion.

With both dividends and augmented dividends, we are trusting managers at publicly traded firms to pay out to stockholders any excess cash left over after meeting operating and reinvestment needs. However, we do know that managers do not always follow this practice, as evidenced by the large cash balances that you see at most publicly traded firms. To estimate what managers could have returned to equity investors, we develop a measure of potential dividends that we term the *free cash flow to equity*. Intuitively, the free cash flow to equity measures the cash left over after taxes, reinvestment needs, and debt cash flows have been met. Its measurement is laid out in Table 3.2.

To measure reinvestment, we will first subtract depreciation from capital expenditures; the resulting *net capital expenditure* represents investment in long-term assets. To measure what a firm is reinvesting in its short-term assets (inventory, accounts receivable, etc.), we look at the

Table 3.2 From Net Income to Potential Dividend (or Free Cash Flow to Equity)

	Measure	Explanation
	Net income	Earnings to equity investors, after taxes and interest expenses.
+	Depreciation	Accounting expense (reduced earnings), but not a cash expense.
−	Capital expenditures	Not an accounting expense, but still a cash outflow.
−	Change in non-cash working capital	Increases in inventory and accounts receivable reduce cash flows, and increases in accounts payable increase cash flows. If working capital increases, cash flow decreases.
−	(Principal repaid – New debt issues)	Principal repayments are cash outflows but new debt generates cash inflows. The net change affects cash flows to equity.
=	Potential dividend, or FCFE	This is the cash left over after all needs are met. If it is positive, it represents a potential dividend. If it is negative, it is a cash shortfall that has to be covered with new equity infusions.

change in noncash working capital. Adding the net capital expenditures to the *change in non-cash working capital* yields the *total reinvestment*. This reinvestment reduces cash flow to equity investors, but it provides a payoff in terms of future growth. For 3M, in 2007, the potential dividend, or Free Cash Flow to Equity (FCFE), can be computed as follows:

	Net income	=	$ 4,010 million
−	Net capital expenditures	=	$ 889 million
−	Change in working capital	=	$ 243 million
+	New debt issued	=	$ 1,222 million
=	FCFE	=	$ 4,100 million

3M reinvested $1,132 million ($889 + $243) in 2007, and the potential dividend is $4.1 billion. A more conservative version of cash flows to equity, which Warren Buffett calls "owners' earnings," ignores the net cash flow from debt. For 3M, the owner's earnings in 2007 would have been $2,878 million.

The cash flow to the firm is the cash left over after taxes and after all reinvestment needs have been met, but before interest and principal payments on debt. To get to cash flow to the firm, you start with operating earnings, instead of net income, and subtract out taxes paid and reinvestment, defined exactly the same way it was to get to free cash flow to equity:

Free cash flow to firm (FCFF) = After-tax operating income − (Net Capital expenditures + Change in non-cash working capital)

Using our earlier definition of reinvestment, we can also write the FCFF as follows:

$$\text{Reinvestment rate}$$
$$= \frac{\left(\text{Net Capital expenditure} + \text{Change in non-cash working capital}\right)}{\text{After-tax operating income}}$$

Free cash flow to the firm = After-tax operating income (1 − Reinvestment rate)

The reinvestment rate can exceed 100 percent,* if the firm is reinvesting more than it is earning, or it can also be less than zero, for firms that are divesting assets and shrinking capital. Both FCFE and FCFF are after taxes and reinvestment and both can be negative, either because a firm has negative earnings or because it has reinvestment needs that exceed income. The key difference is that the FCFE is after debt cash flows and the

*In practical terms, this firm will have to raise either new debt or new equity to cover the excess reinvestment.

FCFF is before. 3M's FCFF in 2007 is computed as follows:

	Operating income after taxes	=	$3,586 million
—	Net capital expenditures	=	$ 889 million
—	Change in working capital	=	$ 243 million
=	FCFF	=	$2,454 million

This represents cash flows from operations for 3M in 2007.

Risk

Cash flows that are riskier should be assessed a lower value than more stable cash flows. In conventional discounted cash flow valuation models, we use higher discount rates on riskier cash flows and lower discount rates on safer cash flows. The definition of risk will depend upon whether you are valuing the business or just the equity. When valuing the business, you look at the risk in a firm's operations. When valuing equity, you look at the risk in the equity investment in this business, which is partly determined by the risk of the business the firm is in and partly by its choice on how much debt to use to fund that business. The equity in a safe business can become risky, if the firm uses enough debt to fund that business. In discount rate terms, the risk in the equity in a business is measured with the cost of equity, whereas the risk in the business is captured in the cost of capital. The latter will be a weighted average of the cost of equity and the cost of debt, with the weights reflecting the proportional use of each source of funding.

There are three inputs needed to estimate a cost of equity: a risk-free rate and a price for risk (equity risk premium) to use across all investments, as well as a measure of relative risk (beta) in individual investments.

- *Risk-free rate:* Since only entities that cannot default can issue risk-free securities, we generally use 10- or 30-year government bonds rates as risk-free rates, implicitly assuming that governments don't default.
- *Equity risk premium (ERP):* This is the premium investors demand on an annual basis for investing in stocks instead of a risk-free investment, and it should be a function of how much risk they perceive in stocks and how concerned they are about that risk. To estimate this number, analysts often look at the past; between 1928 and 2010, for instance, stocks generated 4.31 percent more, on an annual basis, than treasury bonds. An alternative is to back out a forward-looking premium (called an implied equity

risk premium) from current stock price levels and expected future cash flows. In January 2011, the implied equity risk premium in the United States was approximately 5 percent.

- *Relative risk or beta:* To estimate the beta, we generally look at how much a stock has moved in the past, relative to the market: In statistical terms, it is the slope of a regression of returns on the stock (say, 3M) against a market index (such as the S&P 500). As a consequence, the beta estimates that we obtain will always be backward looking (since they are derived from past data) and noisy (since they are estimated with error). One solution is to replace the regression beta with a sector-average beta, if the firm operates in only one business or a weighted average of many sector betas if the firm operates in many businesses. The sector beta is more precise than an individual regression beta because averaging across many betas results in averaging out your mistakes.

In September 2008, the risk-free rate was set to the 10-year Treasury bond rate of 3.72 percent, the equity risk premium (ERP) was estimated to be 4 percent, and the beta for 3M was obtained by looking at the businesses in which 3M operated, as shown in Table 3.3.

Table 3.3   Estimating a Beta for 3M

Business	Estimated Value to 3M	Proportion of Firm	Sector Beta
Industrial & Transportation	$8,265	27.42%	0.82
Health Care	$7,261	24.09%	1.40
Display & Graphics	$6,344	21.04%	1.97
Consumer & Office	$2,654	8.80%	0.99
Safety, Security, & Protection	$3,346	11.10%	1.16
Electro & Communications	$2,276	7.55%	1.32
3M as a firm	$30,146	100.00%	1.29

The value of each of 3M's businesses is estimated from the revenues that 3M reported for that business in 2007, and multiples of those revenues are estimated by looking at what other firms in the business trade at. The resulting beta is 1.29 and the cost of equity is 9.16 percent:

$$\text{Cost of equity} = \text{Risk-free rate} + \text{Beta} * \text{ERP}$$
$$= 3.72\% + 1.29 * 4\% = 9.16\%$$

While equity investors receive residual cash flows and bear the risk in those cash flows, lenders to the firm face the risk that they will not receive their promised payments—interest expenses and principal repayments. It is to cover this default risk that lenders add a *default spread* to the riskless rate when they lend money to firms; the greater the perceived risk of default, the greater the default spread and the cost of debt. To estimate this default spread, you can use a bond rating for the company, if one exists, from a ratings agency such as S&P or Moody's. If there is no published bond rating, you can estimate a "synthetic" rating for the firm, based on the ratio of operating income to interest expenses (interest coverage ratio); higher interest coverage ratios will yield higher ratings and lower interest coverage ratios. Once you have a bond rating, you can estimate a default spread by looking at publicly traded bonds with that rating. In September 2008, we computed an interest coverage ratio of 23.63 for 3M:

$$\text{Interest coverage ratio} = \frac{\text{Operating income}}{\text{Interest expenses}} = \frac{\$5,361}{\$227} = 23.63$$

With this coverage ratio, we see little default risk in the company and give it a rating of AAA, translating into a default spread of 0.75 percent in September 2008.

The final input needed to estimate the cost of debt is the tax rate. Since interest expenses save you taxes at the margin (on your last dollars of income), the tax rate that is relevant for this calculation is the tax rate that applies to those last dollars or the marginal tax rate. In the United States, where the federal corporate tax rate is 35 percent and state and local taxes add to this, the marginal tax rate for corporations in 2008 was close to 40 percent. Bringing together the risk-free rate (3.72 percent), the default spread (0.75 percent), and the marginal tax rate of 40 percent, we estimate an after-tax cost of debt of 2.91 percent for 3M:

$$\text{After-tax cost of debt} = (\text{Risk-free rate} + \text{Default spread})$$
$$\times (1 - \text{Marginal tax rate})$$
$$= (3.72\% + 0.75\%)(1 - .40) = 2.91\%$$

Once you have estimated the costs of debt and equity, you estimate the weights for each, based on market values (rather than book value). For publicly traded firms, multiplying the share price by the number of shares outstanding will yield market value of equity. Estimating the market value of debt is usually a more difficult exercise, since most firms have some debt that is not traded and many practitioners fall back on using book value of debt. Using 3M again as our illustrative example, the market values of equity ($57 billion) and debt ($5.3 billion), and our earlier estimates of cost of equity (9.16 percent) and after-tax cost of debt (2.91 percent), result in a cost of capital for the firm of 8.63 percent.

$$\text{Cost of capital} = 9.16\% \,(57/(57+5.3)) + 2.91\% \,(5.3/(57+5.3))$$
$$= 8.63\%$$

When valuing firms, we have a follow up judgment to make in terms of whether these weights will change or remain stable. If we assume that they will change, we have to specify both what the target mix for the firm will be and how soon the change will occur.

Growth Rates

When confronted with the task of estimating growth, it is not surprising that analysts turn to the past, using growth in revenues or earnings in the recent past as a predictor of growth in the future. However, the historical growth rates for the same company can vary, depending upon computational choices: how far back to go, which measure of earnings (net income, earnings per share, operating income) to use, and how to compute the average (arithmetic or geometric). With 3M, for instance, the historical growth rates range from 6 percent to 12 percent, depending upon the time period (1, 5, or 10 years) and earnings measure (earnings per share, net income, or operating income) used. Worse still, studies indicate that the relationship between past and future growth for most companies is a very weak one, with growth dropping off significantly as companies grow and revealing significant volatility from period to period.

Alternatively, you can draw on "experts" who know the firm better than you do—equity research analysts who have tracked the firm for years, or the managers in the firm— and use their estimates of growth. On the plus side, these forecasters should have access to better information than most investors do. On the minus side, neither managers nor equity research analysts can be objective about the future; managers are likely to overestimate their capacity to generate growth and analysts have their own biases. Studies indicate that analyst and management estimates of future growth, especially for the long term, seem just as flawed as historical growth rates.

If historical growth and analyst estimates are of little value, what is the solution? Ultimately, for a firm to grow, it has to either manage its existing investments better (efficiency growth) or make new investments (new investment growth). To capture efficiency growth, you want to measure the potential for cost cutting and improved profitability. It can generate substantial growth in the near term, especially for poorly run mature firms, but not forever. To measure the growth rate from new investments, you should look at how much of its earnings a firm is reinvesting back in the business and the return on these investments. While reinvestment and return on investment are generic terms, the way in which we define them will depend upon whether we are looking at equity earnings or operating income. With equity earnings, we measure reinvestment as the portion of net income not paid out as dividends (retention ratio) and use the return on equity to measure the quality of investment. With operating income, we measure reinvestment as the reinvestment rate and use the return on capital

to measure investment quality. In Table 3.4, we estimate
the fundamental growth for 3M in September 2008.

The fundamental growth rate of 7.5 percent, estimated for 3M, reflects expectations about how much and
how well the firm will reinvest in the future. We estimate
the expected cash flows to 3M for the next five years in
Table 3.5, using a 7.5 percent growth rate in operating
income and a reinvestment rate of 30 percent.

Terminal Value

Publicly traded firms can, at least in theory, last forever.
Since we cannot estimate cash flows forever, we generally

Table 3.4   Estimating Fundamental Growth for 3M

Growth in earnings	=	Proportion invested	×	Return on investment
Operating income 7.5%	=	Reinvestment rate 30%	×	Return on capital 25%
Net income 7.5%	=	Retention ratio 25%	×	Return on equity (ROE) 30%

Table 3.5   Expected Free Cash Flow to Firm for 3M

	Current	Year 1	Year 2	Year 3	Year 4	Year 5
After-tax operating income	$3,586	$3,854	$4,144	$4,454	$4,788	$5,147
− Reinvestment (30% of income)		$1,156	$1,243	$1,336	$1,437	$1,544
= FCFF		$2,698	$2,900	$3,118	$3,352	$3,603

impose closure in valuation models by stopping our estimation of cash flows sometime in the future and then computing a terminal value that reflects estimated value at that point. The two legitimate ways of estimating terminal value are to estimate a liquidation value for the assets of the firm, assuming that the assets are sold in the terminal year, or to estimate a going concern value, assuming that the firm's operations continue.

If we assume that the business will be ended in the terminal year and that its assets will be liquidated at that time, we can estimate the proceeds from the liquidation, using a combination of market-based numbers (for assets such as real estate that have ready markets) and estimates. For firms that have finite lives and marketable assets, this represents a fairly conservative way of estimating terminal value.

If we treat the firm as a going concern at the end of the estimation period, we can estimate the value of that concern by assuming that cash flows will grow at a constant rate forever afterwards. This perpetual growth model draws on a simple present value equation to arrive at terminal value:

$$\text{Terminal value in year } n = \frac{\text{Cash flow in year } (n+1)}{\text{Discount rate} - \text{Perpetual growth rate}}$$

The definitions of cash flow and growth rate have to be consistent with whether we are valuing dividends, cash flows to equity, or cash flows to the firm; the discount rate will be the cost of equity for the first two and the cost of capital for the last. Since the terminal value equation is sensitive to small changes and thus ripe for abuse, there are three key constraints that should be imposed on its estimation: First, no firm can grow forever at a rate higher than the growth rate of the economy in which it operates. In fact, a simple rule of thumb on the stable growth rate is that it should not exceed the risk-free rate used in the valuation; the risk-free rate is composed of expected inflation and a real interest rate, which should equate to the nominal growth rate of the economy in the long term. Second, as firms move from high growth to stable growth, we need to give them the characteristics of stable growth firms; as a general rule, their risk levels should move towards the market (beta of one) and debt ratios should increase to industry norms. Third, a stable growth firm should reinvest enough to sustain the assumed growth rate. Given the relationship between growth, reinvestment rate, and returns that we established in the section on expected growth rates, we can estimate this reinvestment rate:

$$\text{Reinvestment Rate} = \frac{\text{Expected growth rate in operating (net income)}}{\text{Return on capital (equity)}}$$

Thus, the effect on the terminal value of increasing the growth rate will be partially or completely offset by the loss in cash flows because of the higher reinvestment rate. Whether value increases or decreases as the stable growth rate increases will entirely depend upon what you assume about the return on investment. If the return on capital (equity) is higher than the cost of capital (equity) in the stable growth period, increasing the stable growth rate will increase value. *If the return on capital is equal to the stable period cost of capital, increasing the stable growth rate will have no effect on value.* The key assumption in the terminal value computation is not what growth rate you use in the valuation, but what excess returns accompany that growth rate. There are some analysts who believe that zero excess return is the only sustainable assumption for stable growth, since no firm can maintain competitive advantages forever. In practice, though, firms with strong and sustainable competitive advantages can maintain excess returns, though at fairly modest levels, for very long time periods.

Using 3M, we assumed that the firm would be in stable growth after the fifth year and grow 3 percent a year forever (set at the risk-free rate). As the growth declines after year five, the beta is adjusted towards one and the debt ratio is raised to the industry average of 20 percent to reflect the overall stability of the company. Since the cost of debt is relatively low, we leave it unchanged, resulting in a drop in the cost of capital to 6.76 percent.

The reinvestment rate in stable growth is changed to reflect the assumption that there will be no excess returns in stable growth (return on capital = cost of capital = 6.76%).

$$\text{Reinvestment Rate in stable growth} = \frac{3\%}{6.76\%} = 44.40\%$$

The resulting terminal value at the end of year five is $78,464 million. (The after-tax operating income in year 6 is obtained by growing the income in year 5 by 3 percent.)

$$\frac{\text{After tax operating income in year 6 } (1 - \text{Reinvestment rate})}{\text{Cost of capital} - \text{Expected growth rate}}$$

$$= \frac{5,147(1.03)(1 - .444)}{.0676 - .03} = \$78,464$$

Discounting this terminal value and the cash flows from Table 3.3 at the cost of capital of 8.63 percent yields a value of $64,291 million for operating assets:

$$\frac{2698}{1.0863} + \frac{2900}{1.0863^2} + \frac{3118}{1.0863^3} + \frac{3352}{1.0863^4} + \frac{(3603 + 78464)}{1.0863^5} = \$64,291$$

Tying Up Loose Ends

Discounting cash flows at the risk-adjusted rates gives an estimate of value, but how do you get to value per share?

If you discounted dividends or free cash flows to equity on a per-share basis at the cost of equity, you have your estimate of value per share. If you discounted cash flows to the firm, you have four adjustments to make to get to value per share:

1. *Add back the cash balance of the firm:* Since free cash flow to the firm is based upon operating income, you have not considered the income from cash or incorporated it into value.

2. *Adjust for cross holdings:* Add back the values of small (minority) holdings that you have in other companies; the income from these holdings was not included in your cash flow. If you have a majority stake in another company, the requirement that you consolidate and report 100 percent of the subsidiary's operating income as your own will create *minority interests*, the accounting estimate of the portion of the subsidiary that does not belong to you. You have to subtract out the estimated market value of the minority interest from your consolidated firm value.

3. *Subtract other potential liabilities:* If you have under-funded pension or health care obligations or ongoing lawsuits that may generate large liabilities, you have to estimate a value and subtract it out.

4. *Subtract the value of management options:* When companies give options to employees, analysts often use short cuts (such as adjusting the number of shares for dilution) to deal with these options. The right approach is to value the options (using option pricing models), reduce the value of equity by the option value, and then divide by the actual number of shares outstanding.

With 3M, we add the cash balance to, and subtract out the debt and the estimated value of management options from the value of the operating assets to generate a value of equity for 3M of $60,776 million.

Value of 3M equity = Value of operating assets + Cash − Debt
− Management options
= $64,291 + $3,253 − $5,297 − $1,216 = $60,776 million

If you divide by 699 million—the number of shares outstanding at the time—the result is a value of $86.95 per share.

What Do These Models Tell Us?

What if the intrinsic value that you derive, from your estimates of cash flows and risk, is very different from the market price? There are three possible explanations.

One is that you have made erroneous or unrealistic assumptions about a company's future growth potential or riskiness. A second and related explanation is that you have made incorrect assessments of risk premiums for the entire market. A third is that the market price is wrong and that you are right in your value assessment. Even in the last scenario, there is no guarantee that you can make money from your valuations. For that to occur, markets have to correct their mistakes and that may not happen in the near future. In fact, you can buy stocks that you believe are undervalued and find them become more undervalued over time. That is why a long time horizon is almost a prerequisite for using intrinsic valuation models. Giving the market more time (say three to five years) to fix its mistakes provides better odds than hoping that it will happen in the next quarter or the next six months.

The intrinsic value per share of $86.95 that we derived for 3M in September 2008 was higher than the stock price of $80 at the time. While the stock looks undervalued, the degree of undervaluation (less than 10 percent) is well within the margin of error in the valuation. Hence, I did not feel the urge to buy at the time. A few months later, I revalued the firm at $72, when the stock was trading at $54, and did buy its stock.

It's All in the Intrinsic Value!

The intrinsic value of a company reflects its fundamentals. Estimates of cash flows, growth, and risk are all embedded in that value, and it should have baked into it all of the other qualitative factors that are often linked to high value, such as a great management team, superior technology, and a long-standing brand name. There is no need for garnishing in a well-done intrinsic valuation.

Chapter Four

It's All Relative!

Determining Relative Value

If Dell (DELL) is trading at 17 times earnings, Apple (AAPL) has a PE ratio of 21, and Microsoft (MSFT) is priced at 11 times earnings, which stock offers the best deal? Is Dell cheaper than Apple? Is Microsoft a bargain compared to both Apple and Dell? Are they even similar companies? Relative valuation is all about comparing how the market prices different companies, with the intent of finding bargains.

In relative valuation, you value an asset based on how similar assets are priced in the market. A prospective house buyer decides how much to pay for a house by looking at the prices paid for similar houses in the neighborhood. In the same vein, a potential investor in GM's Initial Public Offering (IPO) in 2010 could have estimated its value by looking at the market pricing of other automobile companies. The three essential steps in relative valuation are:

1. Find comparable assets that are priced by the market.
2. Scale the market prices to a common variable to generate standardized prices that are comparable across assets
3. Adjust for differences across assets when comparing their standardized values.

A newer house with more updated amenities should be priced higher than a similar sized older house that needs renovation, and a higher growth company should trade at a higher price than a lower growth company in the same sector.

Relative valuation can be done with less information and more quickly than intrinsic valuation and is more likely to reflect the market mood of the moment. Not surprisingly, most valuations that you see are relative.

Standardized Values and Multiples

Comparing assets that are not exactly similar can be a challenge. If you were to compare the prices of two buildings of different sizes in the same location, the smaller building will look cheaper unless you control for the size difference by computing the price per square foot. When comparing publicly traded stocks across companies, the price per share of a stock is a function both of the value of the equity in a company and the number of shares outstanding in the firm. To compare the pricing of "similar" firms in the market, the market value of a company can be standardized relative to how much it earns, its accounting book value, to revenue generated, or to a measure specific to a firm or sector (number of customers, subscribers, units, and so on). When estimating market value, you have three choices:

1. *Market value of equity:* The price per share or market capitalization.
2. *Market value of firm:* The sum of the market values of both debt and equity.
3. *Market value of operating assets or enterprise value:* The sums of the market values of debt and equity, but with cash netted out of the value.

When measuring earnings and book value, you can again measure them from the perspective only of equity investors or of both debt and equity (firm). Thus, earnings per share and net income are earnings to equity, whereas operating income measures earnings to the firm. The shareholders' equity on a balance sheet is book value of equity; the book value of the entire business includes debt; and the book value of invested capital is that book value, net of cash. To provide a few illustrations: You can divide the market value of equity by the net income in order to estimate the PE ratio (measuring how much equity investors are paying per dollar of earnings), or divide enterprise value by EBITDA (Earnings before interest, taxes, depreciation, and amortization) to get a sense of the market value of operating assets, relative to operating cash flow. The central reason for standardizing, though, does not change. We want to compare these numbers across companies.

Four Keys to Using Multiples

Multiples are easy to use and easy to misuse. There are four basic steps to using multiples wisely and detecting misuse in the hands of others, starting with making sure that they are defined consistently, and then moving on to looking at their distributional characteristics and the variables that determine their values, and concluding with using them in comparisons across firms.

Definitional Tests

Even the simplest multiples are defined and computed differently by different analysts. A PE ratio for a company can be computed using earnings from the last fiscal year (current PE), the last four quarters (trailing PE), or the next four quarters (forward), yielding very different estimates. It can also vary depending upon whether you use diluted or primary earnings. The first test to run on a multiple is to examine whether the numerator and denominator are defined consistently. If the numerator is an equity value, then the denominator should be an equity value as well. If the numerator is a firm value, then the denominator should be a firm value as well. To illustrate, the PE ratio is a consistently defined multiple, since the numerator is the price per share (which is an equity value), and the denominator is earnings per share (which is also an equity value). So is the enterprise value to EBITDA multiple, since the numerator and denominator are both measures of operating assets; the enterprise value measures the market value of the operating assets of a company and the EBITDA is the cash flow generated by the operating assets. In contrast, the price to sales ratio and price to EBITDA are not consistently defined, since they divide the market value of equity by an operating measure. Using these multiples will lead you to finding any firm with a significant debt burden to be cheap.

For comparisons across companies, the multiple has to be defined uniformly across all of the firms in the group. Thus, if the trailing PE is used for one firm, it has to be used for all of the others as well, and the trailing earnings per share has to be computed the same way for all firms in the sample. With both earnings and book value measures, differences in accounting standards can result in very different earnings and book value numbers for similar firms. Even with the same accounting standards governing companies, there can be differences across firms that arise because of discretionary accounting choices.

Descriptive Tests

When using multiples to value companies, we generally lack a sense of what comprises a high or a low value with that multiple. To get this perspective, start with the summary statistics—the average and standard deviation for that multiple. Table 4.1 summarizes key statistics for three widely used multiples in January 2010.

Since the lowest value for any of these multiples is zero and the highest can be huge, the distributions for these multiples are skewed towards the positive values, as evidenced by the distribution of PE ratios of U.S. companies in January 2010, as shown in Figure 4.1.

The key lesson from this distribution should be that using the average as a comparison measure can be dangerous

Table 4.1 Summary Statistics on Multiples—Across U.S. Stocks in January 2010

	Current PE	Price to Book	EV/EBITDA	EV/Sales
Mean	29.57	3.81	36.27	13.35
Standard error	1.34	0.30	17.04	5.70
Median	14.92	1.51	5.86	1.13
Skewness	12.12	41.64	64.64	68.99
Maximum	1,570.00	1,294.00	5,116.05	28,846.00

Figure 4.1 PE Ratio Distribution: U.S. Stocks in January 2010

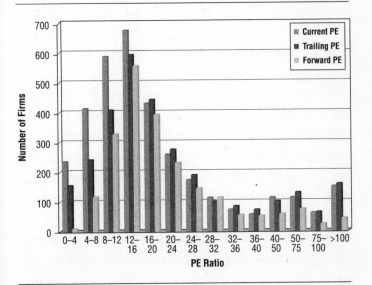

with any multiple. It makes far more sense to focus on the median. The median PE ratio in January 2010 was about 14.92, well below the average PE of 29.57 reported in Table 4.1, and this is true for all multiples. A stock that trades at 18 times earnings in January 2010 is not cheap, even though it trades at less than the average. To prevent outliers from skewing numbers, data reporting services that compute and report average values for multiples either throw out outliers when computing the averages or constrain the multiples to be less than or equal to a fixed number. The consequence is that averages reported by two services for the same sector or the market will almost never match up because they deal with outliers differently.

With every multiple, there are firms for which the multiple cannot be computed. Consider again the PE ratio. When the earnings per share are negative, the price/earnings ratio for a firm is not meaningful and is usually not reported. When looking at the average price/earnings ratio across a group of firms, the firms with negative earnings will all drop out of the sample because the price/earnings ratio cannot be computed. Why should this matter when the sample is large? The fact that the firms that are taken out of the sample are the firms losing money implies that the average PE ratio for the group will be biased because of the elimination of these firms. As a general rule, you should be skeptical about any multiple that results in a significant reduction in the number of firms being analyzed.

Finally, multiples change over time for the entire market and for individual sectors. To provide a measure of how much multiples can change over time, Table 4.2 reports the average and median PE ratios for U.S. stocks from 2000 to 2010. A stock with a PE of 15 would have been cheap in 2008, expensive in 2009, and fairly priced in 2010. In the last column, we note the percentage of firms in the overall sample for which we were able to compute PE ratios. Note that more than half of all U.S. firms had negative earnings in 2010, reflecting the economic slowdown in 2009. Why do multiples change over time?

Table 4.2   PE Ratios across Time: 2000–2010

Year	Average PE	Median PE	% of All Firms with a PE
2000	52.16	24.55	65%
2001	44.99	14.74	63%
2002	43.44	15.5	57%
2003	33.36	16.68	50%
2004	41.4	20.76	58%
2005	48.12	23.21	56%
2006	44.33	22.40	57%
2007	40.77	21.21	58%
2008	45.02	18.16	56%
2009	18.91	9.80	54%
2010	29.57	14.92	49%

Some of the change can be attributed to fundamentals. As interest rates and economic growth shift over time, the pricing of stocks will change to reflect these shifts; lower interest rates, for instance, played a key role in the rise of PE ratios through the 1990s. Some of the change, though, comes from changes in market perception of risk. As investors become more risk averse, which tends to happen during recessions, multiples paid for stocks will decrease. From a practical standpoint, what are the consequences? The first is that comparisons of multiples across time are fraught with danger. For instance, the common practice of branding a market to be under or overvalued based upon comparing the PE ratio today to past PE ratios will lead to misleading judgments when interest rates are higher or lower than historical norms. The second is that relative valuations have short shelf lives. A stock may look cheap relative to comparable companies today, but that assessment can shift dramatically over the next few months.

Analytical Tests

You make just as many assumptions when you do a relative valuation as you do in a discounted cash flow valuation. The difference is that the assumptions in a relative valuation are implicit and unstated, whereas those in discounted cash flow valuation are explicit and stated. In the intrinsic valuation chapter, we observed that the value of a firm is a function of three variables—its capacity to generate cash flows, its expected growth in these cash flows, and the uncertainty associated with these cash flows. Every multiple, whether it is of earnings, revenues, or book value, is a function of the same three variables—risk, growth, and cash flow generating potential. Intuitively, firms with higher growth rates, less risk, and greater cash flow generating potential should trade at higher multiples than firms with lower growth, higher risk, and less cash flow potential. To look under the hood, so to speak, of equity and firm value multiples, we can go back to simple discounted cash flow models for equity and firm value and use them to derive the multiples.

In the simplest discounted cash flow model for equity, which is a stable growth dividend discount model, the value of equity is:

$$\text{Value of equity} = \frac{\text{Expected dividends next year}}{\text{Cost of equity} - \text{Expected growth rate}}$$

Dividing both sides by the net income, we obtain the discounted cash flow equation specifying the PE ratio for a stable growth firm.

$$\frac{\text{Value of equity}}{\text{Net income}} = \text{PE} = \frac{\text{Dividend payout ratio}}{\text{Cost of equity} - \text{Expected growth rate}}$$

where the payout ratio is the dividend divided by net income.

The key determinants of the PE ratio are the expected growth rate in earnings per share, the cost of equity, and the payout ratio. Other things remaining equal, we would expect higher growth, lower risk, and higher payout ratio firms to trade at higher multiples of earnings than firms without these characteristics. Dividing both sides by the book value of equity, we can estimate the price/book value ratio for a stable growth firm.

$$\frac{\text{Value of equity}}{\text{BV of equity}} = \text{PBV} = \frac{\text{ROE} * \text{Dividend payout ratio}}{\text{Cost of equity} - \text{Expected growth rate}}$$

where ROE is the return on equity (net income/book value of equity) and is the only variable in addition to the three that determine PE ratios (growth rate, cost of equity, and payout) that affects price-to-book equity.

While all of these computations are based upon a stable growth dividend discount model, the conclusions hold even when we look at companies with high growth potential and with other equity valuation models.

We can do a similar analysis to derive the firm value multiples. The value of a firm in stable growth can be written as:

$$\text{Enterprise value} = \frac{\text{Expected FCFF next year}}{(\text{Cost of capital} - \text{Expected growth rate})}$$

Since the free cash flow of the firm is the after-tax operating income netted against the net capital expenditures and working capital needs of the firm, this can be rewritten as follows:

$$\text{Enterprise value} = \frac{\text{EBIT} (1 - \text{tax rate}) (1 - \text{Reinvestment rate})}{(\text{Cost of capital} - \text{Expected growth rate})}$$

Dividing both sides of this equation by sales, and defining the after-tax operating margin as after-tax operating income divided by sales, yields the following:

$$\frac{\text{Enterprise value}}{\text{Sales}} = \frac{\text{After-tax operating margin} (1 - \text{Reinvestment rate})}{(\text{Cost of capital} - \text{Expected growth rate})}$$

Table 4.3 summarizes the multiples and the key variables that determine each multiple, with the sign of the relationship in brackets next to each variable: ⇧ indicates that an increase in this variable will increase the multiple, whereas ⬇ indicates that an increase in this variable will decrease the multiple, holding all else constant.

Notwithstanding the fact that each multiple is determined by many variables, there is a single variable that dominates when it comes to explaining each multiple (and it is not the same variable for every multiple). This variable is called the *companion variable* and is key to finding under-valued stocks. In Table 4.4, the companion variables and mismatches are identified for six multiples.

Table 4.3   Fundamentals Determining Multiples

Multiple	Fundamental Determinants
PE ratio	Expected growth(⇧), payout(⇧), risk(⬇)
Price to book equity ratio	Expected growth(⇧), payout(⇧), risk(⬇), ROE(⇧)
Price to sales ratio	Expected growth(⇧), payout(⇧), risk(⬇), net margin(⇧)
EV to FCFF	Cost of capital(⬇), growth rate(⇧)
EV to EBITDA	Expected growth(⇧), reinvestment rate(⬇), risk(⬇), ROIC(⇧), Tax rate(⬇)
EV to capital ratio	Expected growth(⇧), reinvestment rate(⬇), risk(⬇), ROIC(⇧)
EV to sales	Expected growth(⇧), reinvestment rate(⬇), risk(⬇), operating margin(⇧)

Table 4.4   Valuation Mismatches

Multiple	Companion Variable	Mismatch Indicator for Undervalued Company
PE ratio	Expected growth	Low PE ratio with high expected growth rate in earnings per share
P/BV ratio	ROE	Low P/BV ratio with high ROE
P/S ratio	Net margin	Low P/S ratio with high net profit margin
EV/EBITDA	Reinvestment rate	Low EV/EBITDA ratio with low reinvestment needs
EV/Capital	Return on capital	Low EV/Capital ratio with high return on capital
EV/Sales	After-tax operating margin	Low EV/Sales ratio with high after-tax operating margin

Application Tests

Multiples tend to be used in conjunction with comparable firms to determine the value of a firm or its equity. A comparable firm is one with cash flows, growth potential, and risk similar to the firm being valued. Nowhere in this definition is there a component that relates to the industry or sector to which a firm belongs. Thus, a telecommunications firm can be compared to a software firm, if the two are identical in terms of cash flows, growth, and risk. In most analyses, however, analysts define comparable firms to be other firms in the firm's business or businesses. As an illustrative example, if you were trying to value Todhunter International and Hansen Natural, two beverage companies, you would compare them to other beverage companies on pricing (PE ratios) and fundamentals (growth and risk).

If there are enough firms in the industry to allow for it, this list can be pruned further using other criteria; for instance, only firms of similar size may be considered. No matter how carefully we construct our list of comparable firms, we will end up with firms that are different from the firm we are valuing. There are three ways of controlling for these differences, and we will use the beverage sector to illustrate each one.

In the first, the analyst compares the multiple a firm trades at to the average computed for the sector; if it is significantly different, the analyst can make a judgment about whether the firm's individual characteristics (growth, risk, or cash flows) may explain the difference. In Table 4.5, for instance, Todhunter trades at a PE of 8.94, much lower than the average of other beverage companies, but it also has much lower expected growth. Hansen Natural also looks cheap, with a PE of 9.70, but its stock has been very volatile. If, in the judgment of the analyst, the difference in PE cannot be explained by fundamentals (low growth

Table 4.5   Beverage Companies in the United States, in March 2009

Company Name	Trailing PE	Expected Growth in EPS	Standard Deviation in Stock Prices
Andres Wines Ltd. "A"	8.96	3.50%	24.70%
Anheuser-Busch	24.31	11.00%	22.92%
Boston Beer "A"	10.59	17.13%	39.58%
Brown-Forman "B"	10.07	11.50%	29.43%
Chalone Wine Group Ltd.	21.76	14.00%	24.08%
Coca-Cola	44.33	19.00%	35.51%
Coca-Cola Bottling	29.18	9.50%	20.58%
Coca-Cola Enterprises	37.14	27.00%	51.34%
Coors (Adolph) "B"	23.02	10.00%	29.52%
Corby Distilleries Ltd.	16.24	7.50%	23.66%
Hansen Natural Corp.	9.70	17.00%	62.45%
Molson Inc. Ltd. "A"	43.65	15.50%	21.88%
Mondavi (Robert) "A"	16.47	14.00%	45.84%
PepsiCo, Inc.	33.00	10.50%	31.35%
Todhunter Int'l	8.94	3.00%	25.74%
Whitman Corp.	25.19	11.50%	44.26%
Average	22.66	12.60%	33.30%

or high risk), the firm will be viewed as undervalued. The weakness in this approach is not that analysts are called upon to make subjective judgments, but that the judgments are often based upon little more than guesswork.

In the second approach, we modify the multiple to take into account the most important variable determining it— the companion variable. To provide an illustration, analysts who compare PE ratios across companies with very different growth rates often divide the PE ratio by the expected growth rate in EPS to determine a growth-adjusted PE ratio, or the PEG ratio. Going back to Table 4.5, take a look at Todhunter and Hansen, relative to other beverage companies:

$$\text{PEG ratio for Todhunter} = \frac{\text{PE ratio for Todhunter}}{\text{Todhunter's growth rate}} = \frac{8.94}{3} = 2.98$$

$$\text{PEG ratio for Hansen} = \frac{\text{PE ratio for Hansen}}{\text{Hansen's growth rate}} = \frac{9.70}{17} = 0.57$$

$$\text{PEG ratio for beverage sector} = \frac{\text{Average PE ratio}}{\text{Sector average growth rate}}$$
$$= \frac{22.66}{12.60} = 1.80$$

Hansen continues to look cheap, on a PEG ratio, relative to the sector, but Todhunter now looks expensive.

There are two implicit assumptions that we make when using these modified multiples. The first is that these firms are all of equivalent risk, a problem for Hansen, which looks riskier than the other companies in the sector. The other is that growth and PE move proportionately; when growth doubles, PE ratios double as well. If this assumption does not hold up and PE ratios do not increase proportionally to growth, companies with high growth rates will look cheap on a PEG ratio basis.

When there is more than one variable to adjust for, when comparing across companies, there are statistical techniques that offer promise. In a multiple regression, for instance, we attempt to explain a dependent variable (such a PE or EV/EBITDA) by using independent variables (such as growth and risk) that we believe influence the dependent variable. Regressions offer two advantages over the subjective approach. First, the output from the regression gives us a measure of how strong the relationship is between the multiple and the variable(s) being used. Second, unlike the modified multiple approach, where we were able to control for differences on only one variable, a regression can be extended to allow for more than one variable and even for cross effects across these variables. Applying this technique to the beverage company data in Table 4.5, PE ratios were regressed against expected growth and risk (standard deviation in stock prices) as shown here:

$$PE = 20.87 - 63.98 \text{ Standard deviation} + 183.24 \text{ Expected growth}$$
$$R^2 = 51\%$$

The R-squared indicates the 51 percent of the differences in PE ratios, across beverage companies, that is explained by differences in our measures of growth and risk. Finally, the regression itself can be used to get predicted PE ratios for the companies in the list. Thus, the predicted PE ratios for Todhunter and Hansen, based upon their expected growth and risk measures are as follows:

$$PE \text{ for Todhunter} = 20.87 - 63.98(.2574) + 183.24(.03) = 9.90$$
$$PE \text{ for Hansen} = 20.87 - 63.98(.6245) + 183.24(.17) = 12.06$$

These can be considered to be risk and growth adjusted forecasts and both companies look undervalued, albeit by less than our initial comparison would have suggested.

Intrinsic versus Relative Value

The two approaches to valuation—intrinsic and relative valuation—will generally yield different estimates of value for the same firm at the same point in time. It is even possible for one approach to generate the result that the stock is undervalued while the other concludes that it is overvalued. In early 2000, for instance, a discounted cash flow valuation of Amazon.com suggested that it was significantly overvalued, whereas valuing the company relative to other Internet companies at the same time yielded the opposite conclusion. Furthermore, even within relative valuation, we can arrive at different estimates of value depending upon which multiple we use and what firms we based the relative valuation on.

The differences in value between discounted cash flow valuation and relative valuation come from different views of market efficiency or inefficiency. In discounted cash flow valuation, we assume that markets make mistakes, that they correct these mistakes over time, and that these mistakes can often occur across entire sectors or even the entire market. In relative valuation, we assume that while markets make mistakes on individual stocks, they are correct on average. In other words, when we value a new software company relative to other small software companies, we are assuming that the market has priced these companies correctly, on average, even though it might have made mistakes in the pricing of each of them individually. Thus, a stock may be overvalued on a discounted cash flow basis but undervalued on a relative basis, if the firms used for comparison in the relative valuation are all overpriced by the market. The reverse would occur if an entire sector or market were underpriced.

Einstein Was Right

In relative valuation, we estimate the value of an asset by looking at how similar assets are priced. While the allure of multiples remains their simplicity, the key to using them wisely remains finding comparable firms and adjusting for differences between the firms on growth, risk, and cash flows. Einstein was right about relativity, but even he would have had a difficult time applying relative valuation in today's stock markets.

From Cradle to Grave—Life Cycle and Valuation

Chapter Five

Promise Aplenty

~

Valuing Young Growth Companies

IN LATE 2010, GOOGLE (GOOG) attempted to buy a young Internet company called Groupon for $6 billion. At the time, Groupon had been in existence for only a year, had about $500 million in revenues, and was reporting operating losses. The firm clearly had growth potential but there were huge uncertainties about its business model. While Google's bid failed, analysts were nonplussed, unsure about how to value a company with almost no operating history and market price data.

If every business starts with an idea, young companies can range from idea companies often that have no revenues or products, to start-up companies that are testing out product appeal, to second-stage companies that are moving on the path to profitability. Figure 5.1 illustrates the diversity of young growth companies.

Most young growth companies tend to be privately owned and funded by their founder/owner or by venture capitalists. In the last two decades, though, companies in

Figure 5.1   The Early Stages of the Business Life Cycle

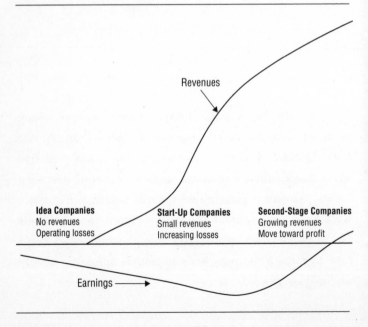

some sectors such as technology and biotechnology have been able to leapfrog the process and go public. When they do go public, they offer a blend of promise and peril to investors who are willing to grapple with the uncertainties that come with growth potential. Young companies share some common attributes:

- *No historical performance data:* Most young companies have only one or two years of data available on operations and financing and some have financials for only a portion of a year.

- *Small or no revenues, operating losses:* Many young companies have small or nonexistent revenues. Expenses often are associated with getting the business established, rather than generating revenues. In combination, the result is significant operating losses.

- *Many don't survive:* One study concluded that only 44 percent of all businesses that were founded in 1998 survived at least four years and only 31 percent made it through seven years.

- *Investments are illiquid:* Even those firms that are publicly traded tend to have small market capitalizations and relatively few shares traded (low float). A significant portion of the equity is usually held by the founders, venture capitalists, and other private equity investors.

- *Multiple claims on equity:* It is not uncommon for some equity investors to have first claims on cash flows (dividends) and others to have additional voting right shares.

While each of these characteristics individually does not pose an insurmountable problem, their coming together in the same firm creates the perfect storm for valuation. It is no wonder that most investors and analysts give up.

Valuation Issues

In intrinsic valuation, estimating each of the four pieces that determine value—cash flows from existing assets, expected growth in these cash flows, discount rates, and the length of time before the firm becomes mature—all become more difficult for young firms. Existing assets often generate little or negative cash flows, and estimating future revenues and discount rates becomes more difficult because of limited or nonexistent historical data. This estimation challenge gets even more daunting when we bring in the possibility that the firm may not survive to become a stable firm and that there may be multiple claims on equity. As a consequence, most investors don't even try to value young growth companies on an intrinsic basis and rely instead on compelling stories to justify investment decisions.

Some analysts try to value young companies using multiples and comparables. However, this task is also made more difficult by the following factors:

- *What do you scale value to?* Young companies often lose money (both net income and EBITDA are negative), have little to show in terms of book value, and have miniscule revenues. Scaling market value to any of these variables is going to be difficult.

- *What are your comparable companies?* Even if a young company operates in a sector where there are many other young companies, there can be significant variations across companies. For young companies in mature sectors, the task will be even more challenging.

- *How do you control for survival?* Intuitively, we would expect the relative value of a young company (the multiple of revenues or earnings that we assign it) to increase with its likelihood of survival. However, putting this intuitive principle into practice is not easy to do.

In summary, there are no easy valuation solutions to the young firm problem.

Valuation Solutions

In this section, we will begin by laying out the foundations for estimating the intrinsic value of a young company, move on to consider how best to adapt relative valuation for the special characteristics of young companies, and close with a discussion of how thinking about investments in these companies as options can offer valuation insights.

Intrinsic Valuation

When applying discounted cash flow models to valuing young companies, we will move systematically through the process of estimation, considering at each stage how best to deal with the characteristics of young companies. To illustrate the process, we will value Evergreen Solar (ESLR), a manufacturer of solar panels and cells, in early 2009. The firm had exploited high fuel prices to some success and showed high growth potential but reported an operating loss of $50 million on revenues of $90 million in the 12 months leading up to the valuation.

Estimating Future Cash Flows   There are three key numbers in forecasting future cash flows. The first is revenue growth, which can be obtained by either extrapolating from the recent past or by estimating the total market for a product or service and an expected market share. The potential market for a company will be smaller, if the product or service offered by the firm is defined narrowly, and will expand if we use a broader definition. Defining

Evergreen as a solar panel company will result in a smaller market than categorizing it as an alternative energy company. The next step is to estimate the share of that market that will be captured by the firm being analyzed, both in the long term and in the time periods leading up to it. It is at this stage that you will consider both the quality of the products and management of the young company and the resources that the company can draw on to accomplish its objectives. Evergreen's management has shown competence and creativity and we will assume that the growth rate in revenues will be 40 percent a year for the next 5 years and then taper down to 2.25 percent in year 10.

A firm can have value only if it ultimately delivers earnings. Consequently, the next step is estimating the operating expenses associated with delivering the projected revenues, and we would separate the estimation process into two parts. In the first part, we would focus on estimating the target operating margin when the firm

VALUE DRIVER #1: REVENUE GROWTH

Small revenues have to become big revenues. How much growth potential does your firm have?

becomes mature, primarily by looking at more established companies in the business. We assume that Evergreen's pre-tax operating margin, currently an abysmal −55.31 percent, will improve to 12 percent, the average margin of more mature companies in the business, over the next 10 years. In the second part, we can then look at how the margin will evolve over time; this "pathway to profitability" can be rockier for some firms than others, with fixed costs and competition playing significant roles in the estimation. The product of the forecasted revenues and expected operating margins yields the expected operating income. To estimate taxes due on this income, consider the possibility of carrying forward operating losses from earlier years to offset income in later years. The net operating loss that Evergreen has accumulated in the past and the losses it is expected to generate over the next three years shelter its income from taxes until the seventh year.

VALUE DRIVER #2: TARGET MARGINS

You can lose money today but, to have value, you have make money in the future. How profitable will your company be, when it matures?

Growth requires reinvestment. With a manufacturing firm, this will take the firm of investments in additional production capacity, and with a technology firm it will include not only investments in R&D and new patents but also in human capital (hiring software programmers and researchers). For Evergreen Solar, the reinvestment is estimated by assuming that every $2.50 in additional revenue will require a dollar in capital invested; this ratio comes from industry averages. In Table 5.1, we estimate the revenues, earnings, and cash flows for Evergreen Solar. The expected cash flows are negative for the next eight years, and existing equity investors will see their share of the ownership either reduced (when new equity investors come in) or be called upon to make more investments to keep the business going.

Estimating Discount Rates   There are two problems that we face in estimating discount rates for young companies. The first is that the market history available is too short and volatile to yield reliable estimates of beta or cost of debt. The second is that the cost of capital can be expected to change over time as the young company matures. To overcome the lack of history, we would suggest an approach that looks past the company and focuses instead at the business the company operates in, and adjusting for key differences. In effect, we use sector averages for discount rates, adjusted for the higher risk of younger

Table 5.1 Expected Revenues, Earnings, and Cash Flows for Evergreen Solar

Year	Revenues	Revenue Growth	Operating Margin	Operating Income	After-tax Operating Income	Reinvestment	FCFF
Current	$90		-55.31%	-$50	-$50	$267	-$317
1	$126	40.00%	-28.39%	-$36	-$36	$29	-$64
2	$176	40.00%	-12.23%	-$22	-$22	$40	-$62
3	$247	40.00%	-2.54%	-$6	-$6	$56	-$63
4	$345	40.00%	3.28%	$11	$11	$79	-$68
5	$483	40.00%	6.77%	$33	$33	$111	-$78
6	$628	30.00%	8.86%	$56	$56	$116	-$60
7	$786	25.00%	10.12%	$79	$73	$126	-$52
8	$943	20.00%	10.87%	$102	$61	$126	-$64
9	$1,037	10.00%	11.32%	$117	$70	$75	-$5
10	$1,089	5.00%	11.59%	$126	$76	$41	$34
11	$1,113	2.25%	12.00%	$134	$80	$18	$62

companies. Thus, in the early years, costs of equity and capital will be much higher for young companies than for more mature counterparts in the same business. To incorporate the changes over time, move the cost of capital toward sector averages, as the young company grows and matures. For Evergreen Solar, the current cost of capital of 10.21 percent reflects a high beta (1.60), a high after-tax cost of debt (8.25 percent), and a debt ratio of 45.64 percent that is unsustainable, given its operating losses. As the firm matures, Table 5.2 illustrates the drop in the cost of capital to 7.20 percent as the beta moves towards one and the tax benefit of debt kicks in.

Estimating Value Today and Adjusting for Survival   Once cash flows for the forecast period have been estimated

Table 5.2   The Dropping Cost of Capital of Evergreen Solar

Year	Beta	Cost of Equity	Cost of Debt	After-Tax Cost of Debt	Debt Ratio	Cost of Capital
1	1.60	11.85%	8.25%	8.25%	45.64%	10.21%
2	1.60	11.85%	8.25%	8.25%	45.64%	10.21%
3	1.60	11.85%	8.25%	8.25%	45.64%	10.21%
4	1.60	11.85%	8.25%	8.25%	45.64%	10.21%
5	1.60	11.85%	8.25%	8.25%	45.64%	10.21%
6	1.48	11.13%	7.60%	7.60%	40.51%	9.70%
7	1.36	10.41%	7.44%	6.85%	39.23%	9.01%
8	1.24	9.69%	7.17%	4.30%	37.09%	7.69%
9	1.12	8.97%	6.63%	3.98%	32.82%	7.33%
10	1.00	8.25%	5.00%	3.00%	20.00%	7.20%

and discounted, you still have to determine what will happen at the end of the forecast period, adjust the value for the possibility of failure, and examine the impact of losing key people in the company.

Terminal Value   The *terminal value* can be 80, 90, or even more than 100 percent of value for a young firm; the more than 100 percent will occur when cash flows are very negative in the near years, requiring fresh capital infusions. The basic principles that govern terminal value remain unchanged: the growth rate used has to be less than the growth rate of the economy, the cost of capital has to converge on that of a mature firm, and there has to be enough reinvestment to sustain the stable growth. Evergreen Solar is assumed to become a mature company after year 10, growing at 2.25 percent a year, with a cost of capital of 7.20 percent befitting its mature firm status, and reinvesting 22.5 percent of its earning to sustain this growth (based on a return on capital of 10 percent forever).

$$\text{Terminal value} = \frac{\text{After-tax operating income } (1 - \text{Reinvestment rate})}{\text{Cost of capital}_{stable} - \text{Stable growth rate}}$$
$$= \frac{80 (1 - .225)}{.072 - .0225} = \$1{,}255 \text{ million}$$

Discounting the expected cash flows for the next 10 years and the terminal value back at the cost of capital yields a value of $192 million for the operating assets today. Adding the current cash balance ($285 million) and subtracting out debt ($374 million) yields a value for the equity of $103 million; dividing by the number of shares outstanding today (164.875 million) results in a value per share of $0.63, significantly lower than the stock price of $2.70 per share at the time of the valuation.

Adjust for Survival   To deal with the risk of failure in a young firm, try a two-step approach. In the first step, value the firm on the assumption that it survives and makes it to financial health. This, in effect, is what we are assuming when we use a terminal value and discount cash flows back to today at a risk-adjusted discount rate. In the second step, bring in the likelihood that the firm will not survive. The probability of failure can be assessed most simply, by using sector averages. Earlier in the chapter I noted a study that used data from the Bureau of Labor Statistics to estimate the probability of survival for firms in different sectors from 1998 to 2005. For an energy firm that has been in existence for one year, for instance, the likelihood of failure over a five-year period would be assessed at 33 percent. These sector averages can then be adjusted for specifics about the firm being valued: the quality of its management, its access to capital, and its cash balances. The value of the firm can be written

VALUE DRIVER #3:
SURVIVAL SKILLS

For young firms to become valuable, they have to survive.
What is the likelihood that your firm will not make it?

as an expected value of the two scenarios—the intrinsic value (from the discounted cash flows) under the going concern scenario and the distress value under the failure scenario. The need to raise capital each year for the next eight years to cover negative cash flows exposes Evergreen to significant risk. If we assume that the likelihood of failure is 33 percent for the firm and that the equity will be worth nothing if that happens, the adjusted value per share is $0.42 ($0.63 * .67).

Key Person Discounts   Young companies, especially in service businesses, are often dependent upon the owner or a few key people for their success. Consequently, the value we estimate for these businesses can change significantly if one or more of these key people will no longer be associated with the firm. To assess a key person discount in valuations, first value the firm with the status quo (with key people involved in the business), and then value it again with the loss of these individuals built into revenues, earnings, and expected cash flows. To the extent that earnings and cash flows suffer when key people leave, the value of the business will be lower with the loss of these individuals, thus leading to a "key person discount." With Evergreen Solar, the value derives more from key technologies than from key people at the firm; hence, there is no need for a key-person discount.

Relative Valuation

Relative valuation is more challenging with young firms that have little to show in terms of operations and face substantial risks in operations and threats to their existence, for the following reasons:

- *Life cycle affects fundamentals:* To the extent that we are comparing a young firm to more mature firms in the business, there are likely to be significant differences in risk, cash flows, and growth across the firms.
- *Survival:* A related point is that there is a high probability of failure in young firms. Firms that are mature and have a lower probability of failure should therefore trade at higher market values, for any given

variable such as revenues, earnings, or book value, holding all else (growth and risk) constant.

- *Scaling variable:* Young firms often have very little revenues to show in the current year and many will be losing money; the book value is usually meaningless. Applying a multiple to any one of these measures will result in outlandish numbers.

- *Liquidity:* Since equity in publicly traded companies is often more liquid than equity in young growth companies, the value obtained by using these multiples may be too high if applied to a young company.

There are simple practices that can not only prevent egregious valuation errors but also lead to better valuations:

- *Use forward revenues/earnings:* Since young firms often have small revenues and negative earnings, one solution is to forecast the operating results of the firm further down the life cycle and use these forward revenues and earnings as the basis for valuation. In effect, we will estimate the value of the business in five years, using revenues or earnings from that point in time. While Evergreen Solar has revenues of only $90 million in the current year, it is projected to have $483 million in revenues in year 5.

- *Adjust the multiple for the firm's characteristics at the forward period:* Consider a simple illustration. Assume that you have a company that is expected to have revenue growth of 50 percent for the next five years and 10 percent thereafter. The multiple that you apply to revenues or earnings in year five should reflect an expected growth rate of 10 percent (and not 50 percent). To estimate a value for Evergreen Solar in year five, we use 1.55, the multiple of revenues at which larger, mature firms in the sector trade at today.

- *Adjust for time value and survival risk:* When forward multiples are used to derive value, we need to adjust for the time value of money and the likelihood that the firm will not survive to get to the forward value. Incorporating the expected revenues for Evergreen Solar, applying the sector average multiple, and adjusting for the likelihood of failure (33 percent):

Estimated enterprise value in year 5 = $483 *1.55 = $749 million

Estimated enterprise value today = $749/1.1021^5 = $457 million

Survival-adjusted enterprise value = $457 *.67 = $305 million

Adding the current cash balance ($285 million) and subtracting out debt ($374 million) yields a value for the equity of $216 million and a value per share of $1.31, a little closer to the current market price of $2.70. However, both the intrinsic and relative valuations suggest that the stock is overpriced.

Are We Missing Something?

In both discounted cash flow and relative valuation, we build in our expectations of what success will look like in terms of revenues and earnings. Sometimes, success in one business or market can be a stepping-stone to success in other businesses or markets.

- Success with an existing product can sometimes provide an opening for a firm to introduce a new product. The success of the iPod laid the foundations for the introduction of the iPhone and the iPad for Apple.

- Companies that succeed with a product in one market may be able to expand into other markets with similar success. The most obvious example of this is expanding into foreign markets to build on domestic market success, a pathway adopted by companies like Coca Cola, McDonald's, and many retail companies. The more subtle examples are products that are directed at one market that serendipitously find new markets: An ulcer drug that reduces cholesterol would be a good example.

Why cannot we build expectations about new products and new markets into our cash flows and value? We can try, but there are two problems. First, our forecasts about these potential product and market extensions will be very hazy at the time of the initial valuation and the cash flows will reflect this uncertainty. Apple would not have been able to visualize the potential market for the iPhone at the time that they were introducing the iPod. Second, it is the information gleaned and the lessons learned during the initial product launch and subsequent development that allows firms to take full advantage of the follow-up offerings. It is this learning and adaptive behavior that gives rise to value that adds to the estimated intrinsic value.

Value Plays

There are many reasons why young growth companies fail: Revenue growth may lag, target margins may be lower than expected, capital markets may shut down, or key people may leave. Investors can

(Continued)

improve their odds of success by focusing on the following:

- *Big potential market:* The potential market for the company's products and services has to be large enough to absorb high revenue growth for an extended period, without being overwhelmed.
- *Expense tracking and controls:* Young companies can become undisciplined in tracking and controlling expenses, while chasing growth. Set targets for margin improvement and view failure to meet these targets as reasons to sell.
- *Access to capital:* Capital access is critical to both growth and success. Look for firms with larger cash balances and institutional investor bases because they are better positioned.
- *Dependence on key individuals:* Young firms are often dependent upon key individuals or founders. Focus on firms that have built up a solid bench to back up key personnel.
- *Exclusivity:* Success will attract competition, often from larger companies with deep pockets. You want young firms that have products that are difficult for others to imitate, whether this exclusivity comes from patents, technology, or brand name. As a bonus, with exclusivity, success is also

more likely to feed on itself, allowing a firm to enter new markets and introduce new products.

In summary, you want to invest in young companies with tough-to-imitate products that have huge potential markets, are working at keeping expenses under control, and have access to capital. Not easy to do, but done right, it is a high risk, high return proposition.

Chapter Six

Growing Pains

Valuing Growth Companies

IN 2001, GOOGLE (GOOG) WAS a young start-up company, with a few million in revenue and operating losses. Over the following decade, the company saw explosive growth, and in 2009, the company reported operating profits of $6.5 billion on revenues of $23.7 billion and had a market value exceeding $200 billion. Google is still a growth company, but it is a much larger one today. The two big questions in valuing it are whether it can sustain growth going forward, and how its risk profile has changed and will continue to change in the future.

So, what is a growth company? There are many definitions for growth companies used in practice but they all tend to be subjective and flawed. Some analysts, for instance, categorize companies as growth companies or mature companies, based upon the sectors that they operate in. Thus, technology companies in the United States are treated as growth companies, whereas steel companies are considered mature. This definition clearly misses the vast differences in growth prospects across companies within any given sector. Others categorize companies trading at high PE ratios as growth companies, trusting markets to make the distinction. Here is an alternative definition: Growth firms get more of their value from investments that they expect to make in the future and less from investments already made. While this may seem like a restatement of the growth categorization described earlier, where firms with high growth rates are treated as growth companies, there is an important difference. The value of growth assets is a function of not only how much growth is anticipated but also the quality of that growth, measured in terms of excess returns: returns on the invested capital in these assets, relative to the cost of capital.

Growth companies are diverse in size and growth prospects, but they share some common characteristics:

- *Dynamic financials:* Not only can the earnings and book value numbers for the latest year be very different from numbers in the prior year, but they can change dramatically even over shorter time periods.

- *Size disconnect:* The market values of growth companies, if they are publicly traded, are often much higher than the book values, since markets incorporate the value of growth assets and accountants do not. In addition, the market values can seem discordant with the operating numbers for the firm—revenues and earnings. Many growth firms have market values in the billions, while reporting small revenues and negative earnings.

- *Use of debt:* Growth firms in any business will tend to carry less debt, relative to their value (intrinsic or market), than more stable firms in the same business, simply because they do not have the cash flows from existing assets to support more debt.

- *Market history is short and unstable:* Even if growth companies are publicly traded, they generally have stock price data going back for only short periods, and even that data is unstable.

While the degree to which these factors affect growth firms can vary across firms, they are prevalent in almost every growth firm.

Valuation Issues

The shared characteristics of growth firms—dynamic financials, disconnects between market value and operating data, a dependence on equity funding, and a short and volatile market history—have consequences for both intrinsic and relative valuations.

If the intrinsic value of a company comes from its cash flows and risk characteristics, there are problems that can be traced back to where growth firms are in the life cycle. The biggest challenge that we face in valuing growth companies stems from changing scale. Even in the most successful growth company, we can expect future growth to be lower than past growth for two reasons. One is that a company that has posted a growth rate of 80 percent over the last five years is larger (by a factor of 18) than it was five years ago, and it is unlikely to maintain that growth rate. The other is that growth attracts competition which, in turn, crimps growth. Questions about how quickly growth rates will scale down going forward, and how the risk and other characteristics of the firm will change as growth changes, are at the center of growth company valuation.

The issues that make discounted cash flow valuation difficult also crop up, not surprisingly, when we do relative valuation and listed next are a few of them.

- *Comparable firms:* Even if all of the companies in a sector are growth firms, they can vary widely in terms of risk and growth characteristics, thus making it difficult to generalize from industry averages.

- *Base year values and choice of multiples:* If a firm is a growth firm, the current values for scaling variables such as earnings, book value, or revenues may provide limited or unreliable clues to the future potential for the firm.

- *Controlling for growth differences:* Not only does the level of growth make a difference to value, but so does the length of the growth period and the excess returns that accompany that growth rate. Put another way, two companies with the same expected growth rate in earnings can trade at very different multiples of these earnings.

- *Controlling for risk differences:* Determining how the trade-off between growth and risk will affect value is difficult to do in any valuation but becomes doubly so in relative valuation, where many companies have both high growth and high risk.

Analysts who use multiples to value growth firms may feel a false sense of security about their valuations, since their assumptions are often implicit rather than explicit. The reality, though, is that relative valuations yield valuations that are just as subject to error as discounted cash flow valuations.

Valuation Solutions

While growth companies raise thorny estimation problems, we can navigate our way through these problems to arrive at values for these firms that are less likely to be contaminated by internal inconsistencies.

Intrinsic Valuation

The discounted cash flow models used to value growth companies need to allow for changing growth and margins over time. Consequently, models that lock in the current characteristics of the company do not perform as well as more flexible models, where analysts can change the inputs. To illustrate the process, we will value Under Armour (UA), a company that offers microfiber apparel for athletes. The company was founded by Kevin Plank in 1996 and capitalized on its success by going public in 2006. Revenues at the firm tripled from $205 million in 2004 to $607 million in 2007; over the three-year period, the company had a compounded growth rate in revenues of 44 percent a year.

Valuing the Operating Assets   The valuation process starts with estimating future revenues. The biggest issue is the scaling factor. The question of how quickly revenue growth rates will decline at a given company, as it gets bigger, can generally be addressed by looking at the company's specifics—the size of the overall market for its products and services, the strength of the competition, and the quality of both its products and management. Companies with larger potential markets with less aggressive competition and better management can maintain high revenue growth rates for longer periods. While the entry of well-funded competitors like Nike will dampen growth, we assume that Under Armour will be able to grow revenues at a healthy rate in the near future—35 percent next year, 25 percent in year two, and then tapering off as the firm gets bigger; the compounded revenue growth rate over the next 10 years will be 12.51 percent.

VALUE DRIVER #1:
SCALABLE GROWTH

The faster you grow, the larger you get. The larger you get, the more difficult it is to keep growing. How good is your firm at scaling up growth?

To get from revenues to operating income, we need operating margins over time. In many growth firms, the current operating margin will be either negative or very low, largely because up-front fixed costs associated with infrastructure investments as well as selling expenses directed towards getting new clients (and future growth) are counted in the current year's expenses. As the company grows, margins should improve. Conversely, some growth companies enjoy super-high margins because they have niche products in markets too small to attract the attention of larger, better-capitalized competitors. As the firm grows, this will change and margins will decrease, as competitors emerge. Under Armour's success with microfiber apparel is a good example; in the initial years, larger players like Nike ignored it but are now introducing their own competing products.

In both scenarios—low margins converging to a higher value, or high margins dropping back to more sustainable levels—we have to make judgment calls on what the target margin should be and how the current margin will change over time towards this target. The answer to the first question can usually be found by looking at both the average operating margins commanded by larger, more stable firms in that industry. The answer to the second will depend upon the reason for the divergence between the current margin and the target margin. With infrastructure

VALUE DRIVER #2:
SUSTAINABLE MARGINS

Success attracts competition and competition can hurt margins. How strong is your company's competitive edge?

companies, for instance, it will reflect how long it will take for the investment to be operational and capacity to be fully utilized. Under Armour currently has a pre-tax operating margin of 12.25 percent, which we see increasing slightly over the next 10 years, primarily from economies of scale, to the industry average of 12.72 percent in year 10.

In keeping with the theme that firms have to reinvest in order to grow, we will follow one of three paths to estimate reinvestment. The first and most general approach is to estimate the reinvestment using the change in revenue and a sales-to-capital ratio, estimated using either historical data for the firm or industry averages. Thus, assuming a sales-to-capital ratio of 2.5, in conjunction with a revenue increase of $250 million, will result in reinvestment of $100 million. For growth firms that have a more established record of earnings and reinvestment, we can estimate the growth rate as a product of the reinvestment rate and the return on capital on these investments. Finally, growth firms that have already invested in capacity for future years are in the unusual position of being able to grow with little or no reinvestment for the near term. For these firms, we can forecast capacity usage to determine how long the investment holiday will last and when the firm will have to reinvest again. For Under Armour, we use the first approach, and use the industry-average sales-to-capital ratio of 1.83 to estimate reinvestment each year. The resulting free cash flows to the firm are summarized in Table 6.1.

Risk Profile Consistent with Growth and Operating Numbers   While the components of the cost of capital are the same for a growth company as they are for a mature company, what sets growth companies apart is that their risk profiles will shift over time. As general rules:

- Growth firms should have high costs for equity and debt when revenue growth is highest, but the costs

VALUE DRIVER #3: QUALITY GROWTH

Growth has value, only if accompanied by excess returns. Do you see your firm generating returns significantly higher than its cost of funding?

Table 6.1 Expected Free Cash Flows to Firm for Under Armour

Year	Revenues	Revenue Growth	Pre-Tax Margin	Operating Income	After-Tax Operating Income	Reinvestment	FCFF
Trailing 12 month	$721		12.25%	$88			
1	$973	35.00%	12.46%	$121	$73	$53	−$65
2	$1,216	25.00%	12.57%	$153	$92	$138	−$41
3	$1,460	20.00%	12.64%	$184	$111	$133	−$22
4	$1,679	15.00%	12.67%	$213	$128	$133	$8
5	$1,846	10.00%	12.69%	$234	$141	$120	$49
6	$1,994	8.00%	12.71%	$253	$152	$92	$71
7	$2,114	6.00%	12.71%	$269	$161	$81	$96
8	$2,209	4.50%	12.72%	$281	$169	$65	$117
9	$2,275	3.00%	12.72%	$289	$174	$52	$137
10	$2,343	3.00%	12.72%	$298	$179	$36	$142
Beyond	$2,396	2.25%	12.72%	$305	$183	$37	$2,730

of debt and equity should decline as revenue growth moderates and margins improve.

- As earnings increase and growth drops, the firm will generate more cash flows than it needs, which it can use to not only pay dividends but also to service debt. While firms are not required to use this debt capacity, the tax advantages of debt will lead some firms to borrow, causing debt ratios to increase over time.

In terms of estimating risk parameters (betas), steer as far as you can from using the limited price data that is available on growth companies; the estimation error is likely to be huge and the company's characteristics will change over time. Instead, use estimates of betas obtained by looking at other publicly traded firms that share the same risk, growth, and cash flow characteristics as the firm being valued. With Under Armour, the beta of 1.30 in the high growth phase, estimated by looking at high growth apparel companies, moves to a beta of 1.00 in stable growth. In conjunction with a drop in the after-tax cost of debt, from 3.75 percent to 2.55 percent, and an increase in the debt ratio from 12.44 percent to 25 percent over the same period, the cost of capital in Table 6.2 declines from 9.27 percent to 7.28 percent.

Steady State: When and what?   The assumptions we make about terminal value loom large with a growth company,

Table 6.2   Cost of Capital Over Time for Under Armour

Year	Beta	Cost of Equity	After-Tax Cost of Debt	Debt Ratio	Cost of Capital
1	1.30	10.05%	3.75%	12.44%	9.27%
2	1.30	10.05%	3.75%	12.44%	9.27%
3	1.30	10.05%	3.75%	12.44%	9.27%
4	1.30	10.05%	3.75%	12.44%	9.27%
5	1.30	10.05%	3.75%	12.44%	9.27%
6	1.26	9.81%	3.51%	14.95%	8.87%
7	1.22	9.57%	3.45%	15.58%	8.62%
8	1.18	9.33%	3.35%	16.62%	8.34%
9	1.14	9.09%	3.15%	18.72%	7.98%
10 and beyond	1.10	8.85%	2.55%	25.00%	7.28%

since it will comprise a much larger portion of the firm's current value than is the case with a mature firm. Assessing when a growth firm will become a stable company is difficult to do, but keep in mind the following general propositions:

- Do not wait too long to put a firm into stable growth. Both scale and competition conspire to lower growth rates quickly at even the most promising growth companies. With Under Armour, the 10-year growth period assumed reflects optimism about the company's growth prospects and competitive advantages; after year 10, the growth rate is assumed to be 2.25 percent, the estimated growth rate for the economy.

- When you put your firm into stable growth, give it the characteristics of a stable growth firm: With discount rates, as we noted in the last section, this will take the form of using lower costs of debt and equity and a higher debt ratio. With reinvestment, the key assumption will be the return on capital that we assume for the stable growth phase.

$$\text{Stable reinvestment rate} = \frac{\text{Stable growth rate}}{\text{Stable period return on capital}}$$

While some analysts believe that the return on capital should be set equal to the cost of capital in stable growth, we would preserve some company-specific flexibility and suggest that the difference between return on capital and cost of capital should narrow during stable growth to a sustainable level. Under Armour's strong brand name is assumed to give them a long-term advantage, translating into a return on invested capital of 9 percent after year 10, in perpetuity. The resulting reinvestment rate and terminal value are reported here.

$$\text{Reinvestment rate} = \frac{2.25\%}{9\%} = 25\%$$

$$\text{Terminal rate} = \frac{183\,(1 - .25)}{(.0728 - .0225)} = \$2,730 \text{ million}$$

Discounting the cash flows over the next 10 years (from Table 5.1) at the time-varying costs of capital (from Table 5.2) and including the present value of the terminal value yields a value of operating assets for Under Armour of $1,384 million.

From Operating Asset Value to Equity Value per Share   To get from operating asset value to equity value per share, add back the cash balance at the company, subtract out debt outstanding, and subtract out management options, before dividing by the number of shares outstanding. For Under Armour, which has $40 million as a cash balance and owes $133 million, the value of equity is $1,292 million. Subtracting out the value of management options ($23 million) and dividing by the number of shares outstanding (49.291 million) yields a value per share of $25.73.

$$\text{Value per share} = \frac{(1384 + 40 - 133 - 23)}{49,291} = \$25.73$$

This estimate is based on the assumption that the shares are all equivalent on dividend and voting rights. Some growth firms continue to be controlled by their founder, who maintains control by holding on to shares with disproportionate voting rights. If that is the case, you have to adjust for the fact that voting shares trade at a premium over nonvoting shares; studies indicate that the premium is about 5 to 10 percent at U.S. companies. Under Armour has 36,791 million class A shares that are held by the investing public and are traded, and 12.5 million class B shares that are held by Kevin Plank. Assuming that the latter sell at a 10 percent premium on the former, we estimate values of $25.09 for the former and $27.60 for the latter. (To compute these values, multiply the number of class B shares by 1.10 and add to the number of class A shares. Dividing the equity value by this adjusted total share number will yield the value for the class A shares.) Since the nonvoting shares were trading at $19/share at the time of this valuation, this suggests that the stock is undervalued.

Relative Valuation

Analysts valuing growth companies tend to use either revenue multiples or forward earnings multiples. Each carries some danger. Revenue multiples are troubling simply because they gloss over the fact that the company being valued could be losing significant amounts of money. Consequently, we would suggest bringing the expected future profit margins into the discussion of what comprises a reasonable multiple of revenues. Forward earnings multiples implicitly assume that the firm being valued will survive to the forward year and that the estimates of earnings for that year are reasonable.

With growth firms, no matter how careful you are about constructing a set of comparable firms and picking the right multiple, there will be significant differences across the firms on both the level and the quality of expected growth, and all three ways described in Chapter 4 can be used to control for differences.

1. *The growth story:* When comparing the pricing of growth firms, analysts often try to explain why a company trades at a higher multiple than comparable firms by pointing to its higher growth potential. In early 2009, for instance, Under Armour traded at a PE ratio of 20.71, well above the average PE ratio of 9.70 for the sector. Under Armour's higher expected growth rate of 20.9 percent (versus 15 percent for the sector) may explain some of the difference, but Under Armour's higher risk (a beta of 1.44 versus the industry average of 1.15) cuts in the opposite direction.

2. *Adjusted multiples:* In the PEG ratio, the PE ratio is divided by expected growth in the future, to estimate a growth-adjusted version of the PE ratio. In effect, a firm that trades at a lower PEG ratio is cheaper than one that trades at a higher PEG ratio. Under

Armour's PEG ratio of just about 1 (20.71/20.90) is higher than the sector average of 0.65 (9.70/15), suggesting that it is overvalued.

3. *Statistical approaches:* When firms vary not only on expected growth, but also on the quality of that growth and risk, the first two approaches become difficult to apply. A multiple regression, with the multiple as the dependent variable, and risk and growth as independent variables, allows us to control for differences across firms on these dimensions. Regressing PE ratios against expected growth and beta for firms in the apparel sector, we obtain:

$$PE = 13.78 + 32.04 \text{ (Expected growth rate)} - 6.60 \text{ Beta}$$

Plugging in Under Armour's growth rate (20.9%) and beta (1.44):

$$PE \text{ for Under Armour} = 13.78 + 32.04 (.209) - 6.60 (1.44) = 10.98$$

At its existing PE ratio of 20.71, Under Armour still looks overvalued. This is at variance with the intrinsic valuation of the company, where the conclusion was that it was undervalued. There are lessons for investors in both conclusions. Long-term investors can draw comfort from the intrinsic valuation, but they should be ready for short-term turbulence, as a result of the relative valuation.

Value Plays

For a growth company to succeed, it has to scale up growth while preserving profit margins. Expected revenue growth rates will tend to drop over time for all growth companies, but the pace of the drop will vary across companies. For investing in growth companies to pay off, here are a few things to look for:

- *Scalable growth*: As a firm becomes larger, growth rates will decline. Focus on firms that are able to diversify their product offerings and cater to a wider customer base as they grow. They will see more growth as they scale up than firms that do not have this capability.
- *Sustainable margins*: As firms become successful, there will be increased competition. Look for firms that are able to preserve profit margins and returns as they grow. Steer away from firms that have to trade off lower margins and returns for higher growth.
- *The right price*: Great growth companies can be bad investments at the wrong price. While multiples such as PEG ratios have their limitations, use them (low PEG ratios) to screen for companies that are cheap.

(*Continued*)

Time can be your ally. Even the most worthy growth company will disappoint investors at some point, delivering earnings that do not match up to lofty expectations. When that happens, there will be investors who overreact, dumping their shares, and embarking on their search for the next great growth story. The drop in price will offer you an opportunity to pick up the company at the right price.

Chapter Seven

Valuation Viagra

Valuing Mature Companies

MATURE COMPANIES LIKE COCA COLA (KO), Hormel Foods (HRL), and General Electric (GE) have been around for generations. They should be easy to value, since they have long periods of operating and market history, with established patterns of investment and financing. But not all long standing practice is good and it is possible that changing the way these companies are run can make a difference in creating higher stock values. Both Coca Cola and Hormel might be more valuable if they used more debt to fund themselves, and GE's value might increase if some of its divisions were spun off as separate entities.

If growth companies get the bulk of their value from growth assets, mature companies must get the bulk of their value from existing investments. If we define mature companies thus, the threshold for being a mature company will vary across markets and across time (the threshold will be higher, when economies slow down as they did in 2008 and 2009, and lower when economies are booming).

The common characteristics of mature companies are:

- *Revenue growth is approaching growth rate in the economy:* While the growth rate for earnings for mature firms can be high, at least in some years, mature firms will register growth rates in revenues that, if not equal to, will converge on the nominal growth rate for the economy.

- *Margins are established:* Mature companies tend to have stable margins, with the exceptions being commodity and cyclical firms, where margins will vary as a function of macroeconomic variables.

- *Diverse competitive advantages:* While some mature firms see excess returns go to zero or become negative, other mature firms retain significant competitive advantages (and excess returns). For instance, Coca Cola uses its brand name to continue to deliver high returns.

- *Debt capacity:* With more cash available for servicing debt, debt capacity should increase for mature firms, though there can be big differences in how firms react to this surge in debt capacity. Some will choose not to exploit any or most of the debt capacity and stick with financing policies that they established as growth companies.

- *Cash build-up and return:* As earnings improve and reinvestment needs drop off, mature companies will be generating more cash from their operations than they need. If these companies do not pay more dividends, cash balances will start accumulating in these firms.

- *Acquisition-driven growth:* As companies get larger and internal investment opportunities do not provide the growth boost that they are used to, one quick fix used by these firms is to buy growth: Acquisitions of other companies can provide boosts to revenues and earnings, though not always to value.

Not all mature companies are large companies. Many small companies reach their growth ceiling quickly and essentially stay on as small mature firms.

Valuation Issues

The biggest challenge in valuing mature companies is complacency. When valuing these companies, investors are often lulled into believing that the numbers from the past (operating margins, returns on capital) are reasonable estimates of what existing assets will continue to generate in the future. However, past earnings reflect how the firm was managed over the period. To the extent that managers may not have made the right investment or financing choices, the reported earnings may be lower than what would be generated under better management. If such a management change is on the horizon, investors will under-value existing assets using reported numbers. A secondary challenge is that mature companies are more likely to turn to acquisitions for growth. As a general rule, the value of acquisition-driven growth is much more difficult to assess than the value of internal or organic growth.

With mature companies, you have a luxury of riches when it comes to relative valuation. You can estimate revenues, earnings, and book value multiples and compare how a company is priced relative to other companies like it, but challenges remain.

- *Too many choices:* The same company can be assigned very different values, depending upon whether we are using a firm or equity multiple, whether that multiple is stated as a function of revenues, earnings, and book value, and the companies we pick to be its comparables. With mature firms, the problem we face is not that we cannot estimate a relative value but that there are too many values to pick from.

- *Management change:* The multiples that we compute of revenues, earnings, and book value reflect the firm as it is managed today. To the extent that changing the management of the firm could change these numbers, we will undervalue badly managed firms with current numbers.

- *Acquisition Noise:* The accounting aftermath of acquisitions—the creation of goodwill as an asset and its subsequent treatment—can affect both earnings and book value, making multiples based on either number dicey.

- *Changing financial leverage:* Mature companies are capable of making large changes to their debt ratios overnight—debt for equity swaps, recapitalizations— and equity multiples, such as PE and price-to-book ratios, will change more than enterprise value or firm multiples as financial leverage changes. A stock buyback, funded with debt, can reduce equity dramatically (by reducing the shares out- standing), but will have a much smaller impact on enterprise value (since we are replacing equity with debt). For the same reason, equity earnings (earnings per share, net income) will change when firms alter debt ratios.

Valuation Solutions

If the key to valuing mature companies is assessing the potential increase in value from changing the way they are run, these changes can be categorized broadly into three groups: changes in operations, changes in financial structure, and changes in nonoperating assets.

Operating Restructuring

When valuing a company, our forecasts of earnings and cash flows are built on assumptions about how the company will be run. The value of the operating assets of the firm is a function of three variables—cash flows from assets in place, expected growth, and the length of the growth period—and each can be altered by management policies.

- *Cash flow from existing assets:* If existing investments are being operated inefficiently, cutting costs and improving employee productivity or redeploying assets to new uses can increase cash flows.
- *Expected growth rate:* Firms can increase their long-term growth by either reinvesting more (higher

reinvestment rate) or reinvesting better (higher return on capital). They can also improve returns on existing assets to generate short term growth. For mature firms with low returns on capital (especially when returns are less than the cost of capital), extracting more growth from existing assets is likely to yield results, at least in the short term. For smaller firms with relatively few assets in place that are generating reasonable returns, growth has to come from new investments that generate healthy returns.

- *Length of the high growth period:* The longer a firm can maintain high growth and excess returns, the higher will be its value. One way firms can increase value is by augmenting existing barriers to entry and coming up with new competitive advantages.

Financial Restructuring

Two aspects of financing affect the cost of capital, and through it the value that we derive for a firm. First, we

---

VALUE DRIVER #1:
OPERATING SLACK

Improving your stewardship of assets can generate large payoffs. What is the scope for improvements in your firm's operations?

will look at how changes in the mix of debt and equity used to fund operations affect the cost of capital. Second, we will look at how the choices of financing (in terms of seniority, maturity, currency, and other features) may affect the cost of funding and value.

The trade-off between debt and equity is simple. Interest expenses are tax deductible and cash flows to equity are not, making debt more attractive, relative to equity, as the marginal tax rate rises. Debt can also operate as a disciplinary mechanism on managers in mature firms; managers are less likely to make bad investments if they have to make interest expenses each period. On the other side of the ledger, debt has three disadvantages. The first is an *expected bankruptcy cost*, since as debt increases, so does the probability of bankruptcy. But what is the cost of bankruptcy? One is the direct cost of going bankrupt, such as legal fees and court costs, which can eat up a significant portion of the value of a firm. The more devastating cost is the effect of being perceived as being in financial trouble: Customers may stop buying your products, suppliers may demand cash for goods, and employees may abandon ship, creating a downward spiral for the firm that can destroy it. The second is an *agency cost*, arising from different and competing interests of equity investors and lenders in a firm. Equity investors see more upside from risky investments than lenders do. As lenders become aware of this conflict of interest, they protect themselves by either writing covenants into loan agreements or charging higher interest rates. Putting this trade-off into practice requires us to try to quantify both the costs and benefits of debt.

In the cost of capital approach, the optimal financing mix is the one that minimizes a company's cost of capital. Replacing equity with debt has the positive effect of replacing a more expensive mode of funding (equity) with a less expensive one (debt), but in the process the increased risk in both debt and equity will push up the costs of both components. The cost of capital approach relies on sustainable cash flow to determine the optimal debt ratio. The more stable and predictable a company's cash flow and the greater the magnitude of these cash flows—as a percentage of enterprise value—the higher the company's optimal debt ratio can be. Furthermore, the most significant benefit of debt is the tax benefit. Higher tax rates should lead to higher debt ratios. Hormel Food's current debt ratio is 10.39 percent. Using the cost of capital approach in Table 7.1 yields an optimal debt ratio of between 20 and 30 percent debt for Hormel in early 2009.

The beta and cost of equity for Hormel Foods rise as the debt ratio increases. The after-tax cost of debt also rises, as the higher debt ratio increases default risk and

Table 7.1   Cost of Capital and Debt Ratios for Hormel Foods

Debt Ratio	Beta	Cost of Equity	Cost of Debt (After-Tax)	WACC
0%	0.78	7.00%	2.16%	7.00%
10%	0.83	7.31%	2.16%	6.80%
10.39% (Now)	0.83	7.33%	2.16%	6.79%
20%	0.89	7.70%	2.16%	6.59%
30%	0.97	8.20%	2.76%	6.57%
40%	1.09	8.86%	3.21%	6.60%
50%	1.24	9.79%	5.01%	7.40%
60%	1.47	11.19%	6.51%	8.38%
70%	1.86	13.52%	7.41%	9.24%
80%	2.70	18.53%	8.89%	10.81%
90%	5.39	34.70%	9.49%	12.01%

the tax benefits fade at debt ratios become higher than 80 percent.

Firms that mismatch cash flows on debt and cash flows on assets (by using short term debt to finance long term assets, debt in one currency to finance assets in a different currency, or floating rate debt to finance assets whose cash flows tend to be adversely impacted by higher inflation) will end up with higher default risk, higher costs of capital, and lower firm values. Companies often use a bewildering array of debt and justify this complexity on the basis of cheapness, defined purely in terms of interest payments. If firms can reduce debt/asset mismatches, default risk can be decreased and firm value can be increased.

> ### VALUE DRIVER #2:
> ### FINANCIAL SLACK
>
> Changing the mix of debt and equity and the type of debt can change value. Does your firm have the right mix of debt and equity and the right type of debt?

Nonoperating Assets

A significant chunk of a firm's value comes from its nonoperating assets—cash and marketable securities and holdings in other companies. While cash and marketable securities are by themselves neutral investments, earning a fair rate of return (a low one, but a fair one given the risk and liquidity of the investments), there are two scenarios where a large cash balance can be value destructive. The first is when cash is invested at below market rates. A firm with $2 billion in a cash balance held in a non-interest-bearing checking account is clearly hurting its stockholders. The second arises if investors are concerned that cash will be misused by management. In either case, investors will discount cash; a dollar in cash will be valued at less than a dollar. Returning cash to stockholders in the form of dividends or stock buybacks will make stockholders better off.

Firms with substantial cross holdings in diverse businesses may find these holdings being undervalued by the market. In some cases, this undervaluation can be blamed on information gaps, caused by the failure to convey important details on growth, risk, and cash flows on cross holdings to the markets. In other cases, it may reflect market skepticism about the parent company's capacity to manage its cross holding portfolio; consider this a conglomerate discount. If such a discount applies, the prescription for increased value is simple. Spinning off or divesting the cross holdings and thus exposing their true value should make stockholders in the parent company better off.

Can Changing Management Change Value?

To examine the interaction between management and value, first examine the effects of changing management on value and then the likelihood that change will happen. If we estimate a value for the firm, assuming that existing management practices continue, and call this a status quo value and reestimate the value of the same firm, assuming that it is optimally managed, and call this the optimal value, the value of changing management can be written as:

Value of management change
$$= \text{Optimal firm value} - \text{Status quo value}$$

The value of changing management will be zero in a firm that is already optimally managed and substantial for a firm that is badly managed. Sub-optimal management can manifest itself in different ways for different firms, and the pathway to value creation will vary across firms. For firms where existing assets are poorly managed, the increase in value will be primarily from managing those assets more efficiently—higher cash flows from these assets and efficiency growth. For firms where investment policy is sound but financing policy is not, the increase in value will come from changing the mix of debt and equity and a lower cost of capital. For Hormel Foods, consider two valuations for the company: The existing management of the company has maintained a high return on capital (14.34 percent) but reinvested very little (19.14 percent), thus generating a low growth rate (2.75 percent). It has also chosen to use relatively little debt (10.39 percent debt ratio) relative to its optimal debt ratio of about 20 to 30 percent. Valuing the company under the status quo yields a value of $31.91 a share. A new management in place, with more aggressive reinvestment (higher reinvestment rate of 40 percent, with a lower return on capital of 14 percent increases growth to 5.6 percent) and financing policies (higher debt ratio of 20 percent) generates a value of $37.80 per share. Thus, the overall value of control is $5.89/share at the company.

There is a strong bias towards preserving incumbent management at firms, even when there is widespread agreement that the management is incompetent or does not have stockholder interests at heart. This bias can be traced to legal restrictions on takeovers, institutional constraints on raising capital to challenge managers, anti-takeover or control clauses in corporate charters, shares with different voting rights, and complex cross holding structures. Notwithstanding these barriers to action, there are companies where the top management is replaced either internally (by the board and stockholders) or externally (through acquisitions). Often, these changes are triggered by pension funds and *activist investors*, who are able to challenge and, in some cases, replace managers. If you take a closer look at these firms, you will notice that management change is more likely to occur at firms with poor stock price and earnings performance, small and independent boards of directors, high institutional (and low insider) stockholdings, and which operate in competitive sectors.

The fact that the Hormel Foundation holds 47.4 percent of the outstanding stock in the company is a key factor. While the foundation is run by independent trustees, it retains strong links with the incumbent managers and is unlikely to acquiesce to a hostile acquisition that will change key parts of the company. Management change, if it does come, will have to be made with the agreement of the foundation. Consequently, we will estimate a probability

VALUE DRIVER #3: PROBABILITY OF MANAGEMENT CHANGE

For value to change, management has to change. How entrenched is management at your firm?

of only 10 percent of the change occurring; in effect, the firm has to be under extreme duress before the foundation will step in and agree to a change.

Assume that you live in a world where management change never happens and that the market is reasonably efficient about assessing the values of the firms that it prices. In this scenario, every company will trade at its status quo value, reflecting both the strengths and weaknesses of existing management. Now assume that you introduce the likelihood of management change into this market, either in the form of hostile acquisitions or CEO changes. If you define the value of the company under existing management as the status quo value and under new management as the optimal value, the stock price of every firm should be a weighted average.

Market value = Status quo value + (Optimal value − Status quo value) * Probability of management changing

The degree to which this will affect stock prices will vary widely across firms, with the expected value of control being greatest for badly managed firms where there is a high likelihood of management turnover.

To the extent that the expected value of control is already built into the market value, anything that causes market perception of the likelihood of management change to shift can have large effects on all stocks. A hostile acquisition of one company, for instance, may lead investors to change their assessments of the likelihood of management change for all companies in the sector and to an increase in stock prices. If you define corporate governance as the power to change the management of badly managed companies, stock prices in a market where corporate governance is effective will reflect a high likelihood of change for bad management and a higher expected value for control. In contrast, it is difficult, if not impossible, to dislodge managers in markets where corporate governance is weak. Stock prices in these markets will therefore incorporate lower expected values for control. The differences are likely to manifest themselves most in the worst managed firms in the market.

Earlier, we estimated two values for Hormel Foods: $31.91 with existing management (status quo value) and $37.80 with more aggressive managers in place (optimal value), and a probability of only 10 percent that management will change. The resulting value is:

$$\text{Expected value per share} = \$31.91(.90) + \$37.80(.10) = \$32.51$$

The actual market price at the time of this valuation was about $32.25. Note that while it is slightly higher than the status quo value of $31.91, the fairer comparison is to the expected value. The stock is very mildly undervalued. It will become even more so if the Hormel foundation sheds or reduces its holdings.

Value Plays

There are two value plays with mature companies. The first is the classic "passive value" strategy that traces its roots to Ben Graham and Warren Buffett, where you invest in "well managed" companies that deliver solid earnings and reasonable growth, but which investors have turned sour on, either in reaction to a recent news event (earnings report) or because these firms are not the flavor of the moment or are boring.

Another way to profit from these companies— and this is a more perverse strategy—is to look for

(*Continued*)

those firms that are poorly managed but could be worth more under better management. To find these companies, consider the following.

- *Performance indicators:* The worse managed a firm is, the greater the potential for increasing value. Look for firms with low operating margins relative to the sector, low returns on capital relative to cost of capital, and very low debt ratios.
- *Potential for management change:* You have to change management for value to increase. Search for companies where the field is not tilted in management's favor (with voting right differences or anti-takeover amendments) and where management change, if not imminent, is at least possible.
- *Early warning system:* If everyone else in the market sees what you do (potential for value and management change), you will not gain much. Focus on firms where there is a catalyst for management change: an aging CEO, a new investor on the board of directors, or a change in the corporate charter.

If you are right in your assessment, you don't have to wait for the management change to happen. The payoff on your investment will occur when the rest of the market recognizes that change is likely and pushes up the stock price to reflect that change.

Chapter Eight

Doomsday

Valuing Declining Companies

IN THE 1960S, GENERAL MOTORS (GM) was the engine that drove the U.S. economy, but in 2009 it was a distressed company facing bankruptcy. Sears Roebuck (SHLD), a company that invented mail order retailing, has been shutting down stores over the last few years as its customers have moved to competitors. As companies age and see their markets shrink and investment opportunities dissipate, they enter the final phase of the life cycle, which is decline. While investors and analysts often avoid these firms, they may offer lucrative investment opportunities for long-term investors with strong stomachs.

Growth companies do not want to become mature companies and mature companies constantly try to rediscover their growth roots. By the same token, no mature company wants to go into decline, with the accompanying loss of earnings and value. So, how would we differentiate between mature firms and firms in decline? Firms in decline generally have little in terms of growth potential and even their existing assets often deliver returns lower than their cost of capital; they are value destroying. The best case scenario is for orderly decline and liquidation and the worst case is that they go bankrupt, unable to cover debt obligations.

Declining companies tend to share common characteristics, and these shared features create problems for analysts trying to value these firms.

- *Stagnant or declining revenues:* Flat revenues or revenues that grow at less than the inflation rate are an indicator of operating weakness. It is even more telling if these patterns in revenues apply not only to the company being analyzed but to the overall sector, thus eliminating the explanation that the weakness is due to poor management.
- *Shrinking or negative margins:* Declining firms often lose pricing power and see their margins shrink,

as they lose market share to more aggressive competitors.

- *Asset divestitures:* Since existing assets are sometimes worth more to other investors, who intend to put them to different and better uses, asset divestitures will be more frequent at declining firms, and especially so if these firms owe money.
- *Big payouts—dividends and stock buybacks:* Declining firms have little need for reinvestment and are thus often able to pay out large dividends, sometimes exceeding their earnings, and also buy back stock.
- *Financial leverage—the downside:* If debt is a double-edged sword, declining firms often are exposed to the wrong edge. With stagnant and declining earnings from existing assets and little potential for earnings growth, debt burdens can become overwhelming.

Valuing declining and distressed companies requires us to balance their declining fortunes with the need to return cash to both their stockholders and lenders.

Valuation Issues

The historical data is depressing, with existing investments generating flat or even declining revenues accompanied by falling margins. In the aggregate, the company may be generating returns on capital that are less than its cost of capital. Rather than investing in new assets, the firm may be shedding assets and shrinking, altering both its asset mix and often its financing mix. As the business and financing mix of the firm changes, its risk characteristics will also change, altering its costs of equity and capital. Even if you overcome these challenges and estimate expected cash flow for a declining firm, you have to consider the possibility that the firm being valued will not make it to stable growth; many distressed firms will default and go out of business or be liquidated. Even if a firm is expected to survive, the expected growth rate in perpetuity may not only be well below the growth rate of the economy and inflation, but also in some cases it can even be negative. Essentially, the firm will continue to exist but get progressively smaller over time as its market shrinks.

Analysts who fall back on relative valuation as a solution to the problems of valuing declining or distressed firms, using intrinsic valuation, will find themselves confronting these estimation issues when they use multiples and comparable firms:

- *Scaling variable:* Earnings and book values can become inoperative very quickly, with both numbers becoming negative; repeated losses can drive the book value of equity down and into negative territory.

- *Comparable firms:* When the other firms in the business are healthy and growing, the challenge is working out a discount for the declining firm relative to the values being attached to healthy firms. In a sector where many or even all of the firms are in decline, not only do your choices of what multiple to use become more limited, but you have to consider how best to adjust for the degree of decline in a firm.
- *Incorporating distress:* Firms that have a higher likelihood of distress will trade at lower values (and hence at lower multiples) than firms that are more likely to make it. That does not make them cheap.

The symptoms of decline caused by too much debt and declining earnings will not disappear just because we base our value on a revenue multiple.

Valuation Solutions

Flat revenues, declining margins, and the potential for distress make valuing distressed companies tricky. In this section, we look at how best to navigate the challenges in both the intrinsic and relative valuation framework.

Intrinsic Valuation

We will build our analysis of declining firms around two key questions. The first is whether the decline that we are observing in a firm's operations is reversible or permanent. In some cases, a firm may be in a tailspin but can pull out of it, with a new management team in place. The second relates to whether the firm faces a significant possibility of distress; not all declining firms are distressed. We will incorporate both conclusions into an adapted version of the intrinsic valuation model. To illustrate the process, we will value Las Vegas Sands (LVS), a casino company that operated the Venetian Casino and Sands Convention Center in Las Vegas and the Sands Macau Casino in Macau, China in early 2009. While the firm does not fit the classic profile of a declining company—its revenues increased from $1.75 billion in 2005 to $4.39 billion in 2008 and it had two other casinos in development—it ran into significant financial trouble in the last quarter of 2008.

In conventional discounted cash flow valuation, you value the business as a going concern and assume that there is only a small probability of bankruptcy or that capital markets are open, accessible, and liquid. If the likelihood of distress is high, access to capital is constrained (by internal or external factors) and distress sale proceeds are significantly lower than going concern values, discounted cash flow valuations will overstate firm and equity value for distressed firms, even if the cash flows and the discount rates are correctly estimated. An alternative to the standard discounted cash flow model is to separate the going concern assumptions and the value that emerges from it from the effects of distress. To value the effects of distress, first value the firm as a going concern, and then estimate the cumulative probability that the firm will become distressed over the forecast period, and the proceeds you expect to get from the sale.

The first step is to value a firm on the assumption that it will stay a going concern. Thus, you estimate expected revenues, operating margins, and taxes for the firm, on the assumption that the firm will recover to health, operating under the constraint that it will be limited in its capacity to reinvest. In making these estimates, you have to be realistic in considering what health will look like for the declining firm: It may very well require the firm to shrink and settle for little or no growth in the long term. When estimating discount rates, you have to assume that debt ratios will, in fact, decrease over time if the firm is over levered, and that the firm will derive tax benefits from debt as it turns the corner toward profitability. This is consistent with the assumption that the firm will remain a going concern. To value Las Vegas Sands as a going concern, we assumed that revenues would grow at paltry rates for the next two years, before new casinos come on line and push up growth, and that pre-tax operating margins would improve over the next 10 years back to 17 percent, the firm's 2006 level. Since the investment in new casinos has already been made, reinvestment needs will be light for the next few years. Finally, as the company reverts back to health, paying down expensive debt, its cost of capital will drop from 9.88 percent to 7.43 percent. The effect of these changes is in reflected in Table 8.1.

To complete the valuation, we will assume that Las Vegas Sands will be in stable growth after year 10, growing at 3 percent a year (set equal to the risk-free rate cap) forever. We will also assume that the return on capital will be 10 percent in perpetuity and that the stable period cost of capital is 7.43 percent.

$$\text{Reinvestment rate} = \frac{g_{stable}}{ROC_{stable}} = \frac{3\%}{10\%} = 30\%$$

Terminal value

$$= \frac{\text{After-tax operating income}_5 \ (1 + g_{stable}) \times (1 - \text{Reinvestment rate})}{(\text{Cost of capital}_{stable} - g_{stable})}$$

$$= \frac{1051 \ (1.03) \ (1 - .30)}{.0743 - .03} = \$17,129$$

Discounting the cash flows in Table 8.1 and adding the present value of the terminal value generates a value of $9,793 million for the operating assets. Adding cash ($3,040 million), subtracting out the market value of debt ($7,565 million), and dividing by the number of shares

Table 8.1 Value of Operating Assets for Las Vegas Sands

Year	Revenues	Operating Margin	Operating Income	After-Tax Operating income	FCFF	Cost of Capital
Current	$4,390	4.76%	$209	$155		
1	$4,434	5.81%	$258	$191	$210	9.88%
2	$4,523	6.86%	$310	$229	$241	9.88%
3	$5,427	7.90%	$429	$317	$317	9.88%
4	$6,513	8.95%	$583	$431	$410	9.88%
5	$7,815	10.00%	$782	$578	$520	9.88%
6	$8,206	11.40%	$935	$670	$603	9.79%
7	$8,616	12.80%	$1,103	$763	$611	9.50%
8	$9,047	14.20%	$1,285	$858	$644	9.01%
9	$9,499	15.60%	$1,482	$954	$668	8.32%
10	$9,974	17.00%	$1,696	$1,051	$701	7.43%

outstanding (641.839 million) yields a value per share of $8.21.

Value/share

$$= \frac{\text{Operating assets} + \text{Cash} - \text{Debt}}{\text{Number of shares}} = \frac{9793 + 3040 - 7565}{641.839}$$
$$= \$8.21/\text{share}$$

The second step is to estimate the cumulative probability of distress over the valuation period. A simple approach to doing this is to use the bond rating for a firm, and the history of default rates of firms in that rating class, to estimate the probability of distress. Researchers have estimated the cumulative probabilities of default for bonds in different ratings classes over 5- and 10-year periods following issuance; these estimates are listed in Table 8.2.

As elaboration, Las Vegas Sands has a rating of B+ and the cumulative default probability for a bond rated B+ is 28.25 percent over the next 10 years.

VALUE DRIVER #1: GOING CONCERN VALUE

Some declining and distressed firms make it back to health. Assuming that your firm is one of them, what will it be worth as a going concern?

Table 8.2   Bond Rating and Probability of Default: 1971–2007

Rating	Cumulative Probability of Distress	
	5 years	10 years
AAA	0.04%	0.07%
AA	0.44%	0.51%
A+	0.47%	0.57%
A	0.20%	0.66%
A−	3.00%	5.00%
BBB	6.44%	7.54%
BB	11.9%	19.63%
B+	19.25%	28.25%
B	27.50%	36.80%
B−	31.10%	42.12%
CCC	46.26%	59.02%
CC	54.15%	66.6%
C+	65.15%	75.16%
C	72.15%	81.03%
C−	80.00%	87.16%

As a third step, we have to consider the logical follow-up question to estimating the probability of distress. What happens then? It is not distress per se that is the problem, but the fact that firms in distress have to sell their assets for less than the present value of the expected future cash flows from existing assets and expected future investments. Often, they may be unable to claim even the present value of the cash flows generated by existing investments. Consequently, a key input that we need to estimate is the expected proceeds in the event of a distress sale. The most

VALUE DRIVER #2: LIKELIHOOD OF DISTRESS

Most declining and distressed firms don't make it back to health. What is the likelihood that your firm will fail?

practical way of estimating distress sale proceeds is to consider them as a percent of book value of assets, based upon the experience of other distressed firms.

The book value of Las Vegas Sands' fixed assets at the end of 2008 was $11.275 billion, but reducing the value by 40 percent to reflect the drop in real estate prices reported for Las Vegas between 2007 and 2008, and dropping it another 10 percent to reflect the need for a quick sale, results in a distress sale value of $6,089 million. Adding the current cash balance of $3.04 billion generates proceeds far less than the face value of $10.47 billion for the debt; thus, the equity investors would receive nothing in the event of a distress sale. While the value per share as a going concern (from a discounted cash flow valuation) is $8.21, adjusting for the likelihood of default of 28.25 percent (based on its B+ bond rating) yields an adjusted value of $5.89.

$$\text{Distress adjusted value per share} = \$8.21\ (.7125) + \$0.00\ (.2825)$$
$$= \$5.89$$

This was about 30 percent higher than the stock price of $4.25 at the time of the valuation.

There is one final consideration that may affect equity value. In healthy companies, you buy equity for expected cash flows: dividends, stock buybacks, or even cash accumulation in the firm. In distressed companies, you invest in the stock for a different reason: the hope that the company will turn its business around and be able to return to health. In effect, the fact that the stock price cannot fall below zero and that equity investors get whatever is left over after lenders have been paid gives equity in distressed companies the characteristics of a call option. In firms with substantial debt and a significant potential for bankruptcy, the option value of equity may be in excess of the discounted cash flow value of equity. The implication of viewing equity as a call option is that equity will have value, even if the value of the firm falls well below the face value of the outstanding debt. This will especially be the case when the firm is in a risky business (risk

VALUE DRIVER #3: CONSEQUENCES OF DISTRESS

In the event of failure, the assets of the firm will be sold and the distress proceeds used to pay down debt. Assuming failure at your firm, what are the consequences?

increases the likelihood that the value of the assets will rise in the future) and has long-term debt (the option has more time to pay off).

Relative Valuation

There are two ways in which relative valuation can be adapted to distressed or declining companies. In the first, you compare a distressed company's valuation to the valuations of other distressed companies. In the second, you use healthy companies as comparable companies, but find a way to adjust for the distress that the firm you are valuing is facing.

To value a distressed firm, you can find a group of distressed firms in the same business and look at how much the market is willing to pay for them. For instance, you could value a troubled telecom firm by looking at the enterprise value to sales (or book capital) multiples at which other troubled telecommunication firms trade. While there is promise in this approach, it works only if a large number of firms in a sector slip into financial trouble at the same time. In addition, by categorizing firms as distressed or not distressed firms, you run the risk of lumping together firms that are distressed to different degrees. Comparing Las Vegas Sands to other casino companies that have very high debt burdens in early 2009, the firm looks overvalued. It trades at 14 times EBITDA, whereas other highly levered casino companies trade at 6.60 times EBITDA. You are implicitly assuming that high debt burdens imply high likelihood of distress and that all these firms are equally exposed to that risk.

Akin to the approach used with discounted cash flow valuation, you can value the distressed firm by highlighting healthy firms in the business as comparable firms and looking at how they are priced. To value the distressed company, you assume that the firm reverts back to health and you forecast revenues or operating income in a future year. You estimate an expected value in the future time period and discount this value back to the present to get a going concern value for the firm. You then bring in the probability of distress and the distress sale proceeds to value the firm today, with both inputs being estimated as they were in the last section. To value Las Vegas Sands using this approach, we first estimate EBITDA of $2.268 billion in year 10, assuming that the firm makes it back to health. Applying the EV/EBITDA multiple of 8.25 that healthy casino firms trade at today, we obtain a value of $18,711 million 10 years from now:

Expected enterprise value in 10 years = $2,268 * 8.25 = $18,711 million

Discounting back to today (at the costs of capital from Table 8.1) yields a value of $7,658 million. In the event of distress, the sale proceeds from asset sales are expected to be only $2,769 million. Adjusting for the probability and effect of distress results in an enterprise value of $6,277 million today.

$$\text{Value today} = \$7,658 \,(1 - .2825) + \$2,769 \text{ million } (.2825)$$
$$= \$6,277 \text{ million}$$

Adding cash, subtracting out debt and dividing by the number of shares results in a value of just over $3.00 per share, below the market price of $4.25.

Value Plays

Investors with long time horizons and strong stomachs can use two strategies with declining companies. The first is to invest in declining companies, where the decline is inevitable and management recognizes that fact. While there will be little price appreciation from your equity investments, you will get large cash flows, as assets are divested and the cash used for dividends and stock buybacks. In effect, your stock will behave like a high-yield bond.

The second is to make a turnaround play, where you invest in declining or distressed companies with the hope that they revert back to health and, in the process, deliver substantial upside. To pull off this strategy, you should consider the following.

a. *Operating potential*: A firm with solid operating assets can become distressed because of its overuse of debt. Search for overlevered firms with valuable assets, in otherwise healthy businesses.

b. *Debt restructuring*: For overlevered firms to recover, there has to be a reduction in the debt burden, coming either from improving operating performance or renegotiation of the debt terms. Look for firms where debt restructuring is being actively pursued and where the likelihood of success is high.

c. *Access to new capital*: Survival becomes much easier if a distressed firm can raise new capital. Focus on firms that have more access to equity or bank financing to improve your odds of success.

If you do invest in distressed companies, your hope is that those companies that manage to turn themselves around will offer high enough returns to cover your losses on the many companies that will fail. Put simply, spread your bets.

Breaking the Mold—Special Situations in Valuation

Chapter Nine

Bank on It

~

Valuing Financial Service Companies

THROUGH THE DECADES, banks and insurance companies have been touted as good investments for risk averse investors who value dividends. Invest in Citigroup (CITI) and American Insurance Group (AIG), they were told, and your investment will be safe. Not only did these firms pay large and stable dividends, but they were regulated. The banking crisis of 2008 revealed that even regulated firms can be guilty of reckless risk taking. While some of these firms may be good investments, buyers have to do their homework, assessing the sustainability of dividends and the underlying risk.

Financial service businesses fall into four groups depending on how they make their money. A *bank* makes money on the spread between the interest it pays to those from whom it raises funds and the interest it charges those who borrow from it, and from other services it offers to depositors and its lenders. *Insurance companies* make their income in two ways. One is through the premiums they receive from those who buy insurance protection from them and the other is income from the investment portfolios that they maintain to service the claims. An *investment bank* provides advice and supporting products for other firms to raise capital from financial markets or to consummate transactions (acquisitions, divestitures). *Investment firms* provide investment advice or manage portfolios for clients. Their income comes from fees for investment advice and sales fees for invest-ment portfolios. With the consolidation in the financial services sector, an increasing number of firms operate in more than one of these businesses.

Financial service firms are regulated all over the world, and these regulations take three forms. First, banks and insurance companies are required to meet regulatory capital ratios, computed based upon the book value of equity, to ensure that they do not expand beyond their means and put their claimholders or depositors at risk. Second, financial service firms are often constrained in terms of where they can invest their funds. For instance, until a decade ago, the Glass-Steagall Act in the United States restricted commercial banks from investment banking activities as well as from taking active equity positions in nonfinancial service firms. Third, the entry of new firms into the business is often controlled by the regulatory authorities, as are mergers between existing firms.

The accounting rules used to measure earnings and record book value are also different for financial service firms than those for the rest of the market. The assets of financial service firms tend to be financial instruments such as bonds and securitized obligations. Since the market price is observable for many of these investments, accounting rules have tilted towards using market value for these assets—*marked to market,* so to speak.

Valuation Issues

There are two primary challenges in valuing banks, investment banks, or insurance companies. The first is that drawing a distinction between debt and equity is difficult for financial service firms. When measuring capital for nonfinancial service firms, we tend to include both debt and equity. With a financial service firm, debt has a different connotation. Debt to a bank is raw material, something to be molded into other products that can then be sold at a higher price and yield a profit. In fact, the definition of what comprises debt also is murkier with a financial service firm than it is with a nonfinancial service firm, since deposits made by customers into their checking accounts at a bank technically meet the criteria for debt. Consequently, capital at financial service firms has to be narrowly defined as including only equity capital, a definition reinforced by the regulatory authorities, who evaluate the equity capital ratios of banks and insurance firms.

Defining cash flow for a bank is also difficult, even if it is defined as cash flows to equity. Measuring net capital expenditures and working capital can be problematic. Unlike manufacturing firms that invest in plant, equipment, and other fixed assets, financial service firms invest primarily in intangible assets such as brand name and human capital. Consequently, their investments for future growth often are treated as operating expenses in accounting statements. If we define working capital as the difference between current assets and current liabilities, a large proportion of a bank's balance sheet would fall into one or the other of these categories. Changes in this number can be both large and volatile and may have no relationship to reinvestment for future growth.

The same issues rear their head in relative valuation. Multiples based upon enterprise value are very difficult, if not impossible, to compute for financial service firms. Controlling for differences in growth and risk is also more difficult, largely because accounting statements are opaque.

Valuation Solutions

If you cannot clearly delineate how much a financial service firm owes and what its cash flows are, how can you ever get an estimate of value? We deploy the same techniques in both intrinsic and relative valuation to overcome these problems: We value equity (rather than the firm) and use dividends, the only observable cash flow.

Intrinsic Valuation

If you accept the propositions that capital at a bank should be narrowly defined to include only equity, and that cash flows to equity are difficult (if not impossible) to compute because net capital expenditures and working capital cannot be defined, you are left with only one option: the *dividend discount model*. While we spend the bulk of this section talking about using dividends, we also present two other alternatives. One is to adapt the free cash flow to equity measure to define reinvestment as the increased regulatory capital required to sustain growth. The other is to keep the focus on what financial service firms generate as a return on equity, relative to the cost of equity, and to value these excess returns.

Dividend Discount Models   In the basic dividend discount model, the value of a stock is the present value of the expected dividends on that stock. For a stable growth dividend-paying firm, the value of a stock can be written as follows:

$$\text{Value of equity} = \frac{\text{Expected dividends next year}}{\text{Cost of equity} - \text{Expected growth rate}}$$

In the more general case, where dividends are growing at a rate that is not expected to be sustainable or constant forever during a period, we can still value the stock in two pieces: the present value (PV) of dividends during the high growth phase, and the present value of the price at the end of the period, assuming perpetual growth. The dividend discount model is intuitive and has deep roots in equity valuation, and there are three sets of inputs in the dividend discount model that determine the value of equity. The first is the cost of equity that we use to discount cash flows, with the possibility that the cost may vary across time, at least for some firms. The second is the proportion of earnings that we assume will be paid out in dividends; this is the dividend payout ratio, and higher payout ratios will translate into more dividends for any given level of earnings. The third is the expected growth rate in dividends over time, which will be a function of the earnings growth rate and the accompanying payout ratio. In addition to estimating each set of inputs well, we also need to ensure that the inputs are consistent with each other.

There are three estimation notes that we need to keep in mind, when making estimates of the cost of equity for a financial service firm.

- *Use sector betas:* The large numbers of publicly traded firms in this domain should make estimating sector betas much easier.
- *Adjust for regulatory and business risk:* To reflect regulatory differences, define the sector narrowly; thus, look at the average beta across banks with similar business models. Financial service firms that expand into riskier businesses—securitization, trading, and investment banking—should have

different (and higher) betas for these segments, and the beta for the company should reflect this higher risk.

- *Consider the relationship between risk and growth:* Expect high growth banks to have higher betas (and costs of equity) than mature banks. In valuing such banks, start with higher costs of equity, but as you reduce growth, also reduce betas and costs of equity.

Consider a valuation of Wells Fargo (WFC), one of the largest commercial banks in the United States, in October 2008. To estimate the cost of equity for the bank, we used a beta of 1.20, reflecting the average beta across large money-center commercial banks at the time, a risk-free rate of 3.6 percent, and an equity risk premium of 5 percent.

$$\text{Cost of equity} = 3.6\% + 1.2(5\%) = 9.6\%$$

There is one final point that bears emphasizing here. The average beta across banks reflects the regulatory constraints that they operated under during that period. Since this valuation was done 4 weeks into the worst banking crisis of the last 50 years, there is a real chance that regulatory changes in the future can change the riskiness (and the betas) for banks.

VALUE DRIVER #1: EQUITY RISK

While financial service firms may all be regulated, they are not equally risky. How does your firm's risk profile compare to that of the average firm in the sector?

There is an inherent trade-off between dividends and growth. When a company pays a larger segment of its earnings as dividends, it is reinvesting less and should thus grow more slowly. With financial service firms, this link is reinforced by the fact that the activities of these firms are subject to regulatory capital constraints; banks and insurance companies have to maintain equity (in book value terms) at specified percentages of their activities. When a company is paying out more in dividends, it is retaining less in earnings; the book value of equity increases by the retained earnings. In recent years, in keeping with a trend that is visible in other sectors as well, financial service firms have increased stock buy-backs as a way of returning cash to stockholders. In this context, focusing purely on dividends paid can provide a misleading picture of the cash returned to stockholders. An obvious solution is to add the stock buybacks each year to the dividends paid and to compute the composite payout ratio. If we do so, however, we should look at the number over several years, since stock buybacks vary widely across time—a buyback of billions in one year may be followed by three years of relatively meager buybacks, for instance.

To ensure that assumptions about dividends, earnings, and growth are internally consistent, we have to bring in a measure of how well the retained equity is reinvested; the return on equity is the variable that ties together payout ratios and expected growth.

$$\text{Expected growth in earnings} = \text{Return on equity}$$
$$* (1 - \text{Dividend payout ratio})$$

The linkage between return on equity, growth, and dividends is therefore critical in determining value in a financial service firm. At the risk of hyperbole, the key number in valuing a bank is not dividends, earnings, or expected growth, but what we believe it will earn as *return on equity in the long term*. That number, in conjunction with payout ratios, will help in determining growth. Returning to the October 2008 valuation of Wells Fargo, the bank had reported an average return on equity of 17.56 percent in the trailing 12 months. We assumed that regulatory capital ratios would rise, as a result of the crisis, by about 30 percent, thus reducing the return on equity to 13.51 percent:

$$\text{Expected ROE} = \frac{\text{Current ROE}}{(1 + \% \text{ Increase in capital})} = \frac{17.56\%}{(1 + .30)} = 13.51\%$$

Wells Fargo paid 54.63 percent of its earnings as dividends in the trailing 12 months. Assuming that payout ratio remains unchanged, the estimated growth rate in earnings for Wells Fargo, for the next five years, is 6.13 percent:

$$\text{Expected growth rate} = 13.51\%(1 - .5463) = 6.13\%$$

Table 9.1 reports Wells Fargo forecasted earnings and dividends per share for the next five years.

Table 9.1   Expected Earnings and Dividends for Wells Fargo in October 2009

Year	Earnings per Share	Expected Growth	Payout Ratio	Return on Equity	Dividends per Share
Trailing 12 months	$2.16		54.63%	17.56%	$1.18
1	$2.29	6.13%	54.63%	13.51%	$1.25
2	$2.43	6.13%	54.63%	13.51%	$1.33
3	$2.58	6.13%	54.63%	13.51%	$1.41
4	$2.74	6.13%	54.63%	13.51%	$1.50
5	$2.91	6.13%	54.63%	13.51%	$1.59

This linkage between growth, payout, and ROE is also useful when we get to stable growth, since the payout ratio that we use in stable growth, to estimate the terminal value, should be:

$$\text{Payout ratio in stable growth} = 1 - \frac{\text{Expected growth rate}}{\text{Stable period ROE}}$$

The risk of the firm should also adjust to reflect the stable growth assumption. In particular, if betas are used to estimate the cost of equity, they should converge towards one in stable growth. With Wells Fargo, we assume that the expected growth rate in perpetuity after year 5 is 3 percent, that the beta drops to one in stable growth (resulting in a cost of equity of 8.60 percent), and that the return on equity in stable growth is also 8.60 percent.

$$\text{Payout ratio in stable growth} = 1 - \frac{3.00\%}{8.60\%} = 65.12\%$$

$$\text{Terminal } price = \frac{\text{EPS in year 6} * \text{Stable payout ratio}}{\text{Cost of equity} - \text{Expected growth rate}}$$

$$= \frac{2.91(1.03)(.6512)}{(.086 - .03)} = \$34.83$$

VALUE DRIVER #2:
QUALITY OF GROWTH

Growth can add, destroy or do nothing for value. What return on equity do you see your firm generating, as it pursues growth?

Discounting the expected dividends for the next 5 years (from Table 9.1), and the terminal price back at the current cost of equity of 9.60 percent, yields a value per share of $27.74, slightly less than the prevailing price at the time.

Cash Flow to Equity Models   Earlier in the chapter, we looked at the difficulty in estimating cash flows when net capital expenditures and noncash working capital cannot be easily identified. It is possible, however, to estimate cash flows to equity for financial service firms, if you define reinvestment differently. With financial service firms, the reinvestment generally is in regulatory capital; this is the capital as defined by the regulatory authorities, which, in turn, determines the limits on future growth. To estimate the reinvestment in regulatory capital, we need to define two parameters. The first is the target *book equity capital ratio* that the bank aspires to reach; this will be heavily influenced by regulatory requirements but will also reflect choices made by the bank's management. Conservative banks may choose to maintain higher capital ratios than required by regulatory authorities, whereas aggressive banks may push towards the regulatory constraints.

To illustrate, assume that you are valuing a bank that has $100 million in loans outstanding and a book value of equity of $6 million. Assume that this bank expects to make $5 million in net income next year and would like to grow its loan base by 10 percent over the year, while also increasing its regulatory capital ratio to 7 percent We can compute the cash flow to equity thus:

Net income   = $5.00 million
Reinvestment   = $1.70 million (7% of $110 million − $6 million)
Cash flow to equity = $3.30 million

This cash flow to equity can be considered a potential dividend and replace dividends in the dividend discount

VALUE DRIVER #3: REGULATORY BUFFERS

Shortfalls (safety buffers) in regulatory capital can affect future dividends. How does your firm's capital ratio measure up against regulatory (and it's own) requirements?

model. Generalizing from this example, banks that have regulatory capital shortfalls should be worth less than banks that have built up safety buffers, since the former will need to reinvest more to get capital ratios back to target levels.

Excess Return Models The third approach to valuing financial service firms is to use an excess return model, where excess returns are defined as the difference between ROE and the cost of equity. In such a model, the value of equity in a firm can be written as the sum of the book value of equity the value added by expected excess returns to equity investors from these and future investments.

Value of equity = Equity capital invested currently + Present value of expected excess returns to equity investors

The most interesting aspect of this model is its focus on excess returns. A firm that invests its equity and earns just the fair-market rate of return on these investments should see the market value of its equity converge on the equity capital currently invested in it. A firm that earns a below-market return on its equity investments will see its equity market value dip below the equity capital currently invested. The two key inputs into the excess return model are the return on equity and the cost of equity.

$$\text{Excess equity return} = (\text{Return on equity} - \text{Cost of equity})$$
$$(\text{Equity capital invested})$$

Framing the value of financial service firms in terms of excess returns also provides insight into the risk/return tradeoff that they face. Faced with low returns on equity in traditional banking, many banks have expanded into trading, investment banking, real estate, and private equity. The benefits of moving into new businesses that offer higher returns on equity can be partly or completely offset by the higher risk in these businesses. To analyze a bank you need to look at both sides of the ledger: the return on equity the bank generates on its activities and the risk it is exposed to as a consequence. The excess returns approach also provides a framework for measuring the effects of regulatory changes on value. Increases in regulatory capital requirements will reduce return on equity and by extension, excess returns and values at banks.

We can frame the Wells Fargo valuation in excess returns terms. The book value of equity at Wells Fargo in October 2008 was $47.63 billion. The present value of excess returns, assuming that it can maintain its current return on equity of 13.51 percent and cost of equity of

9.60 percent forever, is approximately $58.22 billion. Adding this to the book value yields a value for equity of $105.85 billion and a value per share of $28.38 per share, very close to the estimate we obtained in the dividend discount model.

Relative Valuation

In keeping with our emphasis on equity valuation for financial service firms, the multiples that we will work with to analyze financial service firms are equity multiples—PE ratios and price-to-book ratios.

The PE ratio for a bank or insurance company is measured the same as it is for any other firm, by dividing the current price by earnings per share. As with other firms, the PE ratio should be higher for financial service firms with higher expected growth rates in earnings, higher payout ratios, and lower costs of equity. An issue that is specific to financial service firms is the use of provisions for expected expenses. For instance, banks routinely set aside provisions for bad loans. These provisions reduce the reported income and affect the reported price/earnings ratio. Consequently, banks that are more conservative about categorizing bad loans will report lower earnings, whereas banks that are less conservative will report higher earnings. Another consideration in the use of earnings multiples is the diversification of financial service firms into multiple businesses. The multiple that an investor is willing to pay for a dollar in earnings from commercial lending should be very different from the multiple that the same investor is willing to pay for a dollar in earnings from trading. When a firm is in many businesses with different risk, growth, and return characteristics, it is very difficult to find truly comparable firms and to compare the multiples of earnings paid across firms.

The price-to-book-value ratio for a financial service firm is the ratio of the price per share to the book value of equity per share. Other things remaining equal, higher growth rates in earnings, higher payout ratios, lower costs of equity, and higher returns on equity should all result in higher price to book ratios, with return on equity being the dominant variable. If anything, the strength of the relationship between price to book ratios and returns on equity should be stronger for financial service firms than for other firms, because the book value of equity is much more likely to track the market value of existing assets. While emphasizing the relationship between price to book ratios and returns on equity, don't ignore the other fundamentals. For instance, banks vary in terms of risk, and we would expect for any given return on equity that riskier banks should have lower price to book value ratios. Similarly, banks with much greater potential for growth should have much higher price-to-book ratios, for any given level of the other fundamentals.

Assume that you were looking at Tompkins Financial (TMP), a small bank trading at 2.75 times book value in early 2009. That was well above the median value of 1.13 for price-to-book ratios for small banks at the time. However, Tompkins Financial also has a much higher return on equity (27.98%) and lower risk (standard deviation = 27.89%) than the median small bank, both of which should allow the firm to trade at a higher multiple. Using a technique adopted in prior chapters, the price-to-book ratio is regressed against ROE, growth, and standard deviation.

$$PBV = 1.527 + 8.63 \text{ (ROE)} - 2.63 \text{ (Standard deviation)} \quad R^2 = 31\%$$

Plugging in the ROE (27.98%) and standard deviation (27.89%) for Tompkins into this regression:

$$PBV \text{ for Tompkins} = 1.527 + 8.63(.2798) - 2.63(.2789) = 1.95$$

After adjusting for its higher ROE and lower risk, Tompkins still looks overvalued.

Value Plays

Investing in financial service companies has historically been viewed as a conservative strategy for investors who wanted high dividends and pre-ferred price stability. Investing in these firms today requires a more nuanced strategy that goes beyond looking at the dividend yield and current earnings, and looks at potential risk in these firms by examin-ing the following.

- *Capitalization buffer:* Most financial service firms are governed by regulatory requirements on capital. Look for firms that not only meet but also beat regulatory capital requirements.
- *Operating risk:* Risk can vary widely across finan-cial service firms within a sector (banks, insurance companies). Seek out firms that are operating in average risk or below average risk businesses, while generating healthy earnings.
- *Transparency:* Transparency in reporting allows investors to make better assessments of value, and the failure to be transparent may be a deliberate attempt to hide risk. Search for firms that provide details about their operations and the risks that they may be exposed to.
- *Significant restrictions on new entrants into the business:* High returns on equity are a key factor

determining value. Look for firms that operate in profitable businesses with significant barriers to new entrants.

In summary, invest in financial service firms that not only deliver high dividends, but also generate high returns on equity from relatively safe investments. Avoid financial service firms that overreach—investing in riskier, higher growth businesses—without setting aside sufficient regulatory capital buffers.

Chapter Ten

Roller-Coaster Investing

~

Valuing Cyclical and Commodity Companies

WHAT WAS TOYOTA MOTORS WORTH IN 2007, when the global economy was booming and the firm was profitable? What about two years later, at the height of a recession? If oil prices are expected to surge, how much will Exxon Mobil's stock price go up? Uncertainty and volatility are endemic to valuation, but cyclical and commodity companies have volatility thrust upon them by external factors—ups and downs of the economy and movements in commodity prices. Even mature cyclical and commodity companies have volatile earnings and cash flows, making investing in them akin to riding a roller coaster.

There are two groups of companies that we look at in this chapter. The first group, drawn from sectors such as housing and automobiles, includes cyclical companies, with earnings that track overall economic growth. The second group includes commodity companies that derive their earnings from producing commodities that may become inputs to other companies in the economy (oil, iron ore) or be desired as investments in their own right (gold, platinum, diamonds).

Both types of companies share some common characteristics that can affect how they are valued.

- *The economic/commodity price cycle:* Cyclical companies are at the mercy of the economic cycle. The odds are high that most cyclical companies will see revenues decrease in the face of a significant economic downturn and rise when the economy recovers. Commodity companies are, for the most part, price takers. When commodity prices are on an upswing, all companies that produce that commodity benefit, whereas during a downturn, even the best companies in the business will see earnings decline.

- *Finite resources:* With commodity companies, there is another shared characteristic. There is a finite quantity of natural resources on the planet. When valuing commodity companies, this will not only play a role in what our forecasts of future commodity prices will be but may also operate as a constraint on our normal practice of assuming perpetual growth (in our terminal value computations).

When valuing commodity and cyclical companies, we have to grapple with the consequences of economic and commodity price cycles and how shifts in these cycles will affect revenues and earnings. We also have to come up with ways of dealing with the possibility of distress, induced not by bad management decisions or firm specific choices, but by macroeconomic forces.

Valuation Issues

In valuing commodity and cyclical companies, the inputs are heavily affected by macro economic variables—the price of the commodity in the case of commodity companies and the state of the economy for cyclical firms. As commodity prices and economic growth rates change, operating income will change by more, because of the high fixed costs at these firms. Thus, commodity companies may have to keep mines (mining), reserves (oil), and fields (agricultural) operating even during low points in price cycles, because the costs of shutting down and reopening operations can be prohibitive. This volatility in earnings will feed into both equity and debt values (thus affecting cost of capital) and potentially put even the healthiest firms at risk of distress and default, if the macro economic move is very negative.

The same factors will also play out in relative valuations. Multiples of earnings will swing widely for cyclical and commodity companies. While growth potential can vary across companies, growth rates can also change dramatically across the cycle.

Valuation Solutions

The easiest way to value cyclical and commodity companies is to look past the year-to-year swings in earnings and cash flows and to look for a smoothed out number underneath. There are usually three standard techniques that are employed for normalizing earnings and cash flows of cyclical companies.

1. *Absolute average over time:* The most common approach used to normalize earnings is to average them over time. The averaging should occur over a period long enough to cover an entire cycle; the typical economic cycle in the United States lasts 5 to 10 years. This is a simple approach, but using an absolute value will yield too low a number for a growing company.

2. *Relative average over time:* A simple solution to the scaling problem is to compute averages for a scaled version of the variable over time. In effect, you can average profit margins over time, instead of actual profits, and apply the average profit margin to revenues in the most recent period to estimate normalized earnings.

3. *Sector averages:* For firms with limited or unreliable history, it may make more sense to look at sector averages in order to normalize. Thus, you can compute operating margins for all steel companies across the cycle and use the average margin to estimate operating income for an individual steel company. Sector margins tend to be less volatile than individual company margins, but this approach will also fail to incorporate the characteristics that may lead a firm to be different from the rest of the sector.

To see normalization in action, consider a valuation of Toyota (TM) in early 2009, when it was still considered the best-run automobile company in the world. However, the firm was not immune to the ebbs and flows of the global economy and reported a loss in the last quarter of 2008, a precursor to much lower and perhaps negative earnings in its April 2008 to March 2009 fiscal year. Applying the average pre-tax operating margin of 7.33 percent earned by Toyota from 1998 to 2009 to its trailing 12-month revenues of 226,613 billion yen yields an estimate of normalized earnings.

$$\text{Normalized operating income} = 226{,}613 * .0733$$
$$= 1{,}660.7 \text{ billion yen}$$

Assuming that Toyota is a mature company with a stable growth rate of 1.5 percent and a return on capital of 5.09 percent, set equal to its cost of capital in stable growth, allows us to estimate the value of operating assets today as 19,640 billion yen.

$$\frac{\text{Operating income } (1+g)\,(1-\text{Tax rate})\left(1 - \dfrac{\text{Growth rate}}{\text{Return on capital}}\right)}{(\text{Cost of capital} - \text{Growth rate})}$$

$$\frac{1660.7\,(1.015)\,(1-.407)\left(1 - \dfrac{.015}{.0509}\right)}{(.0509 - .015)} = 19{,}640 \text{ billion yen}$$

Adding the value of cash (2,288 billion yen) and cross holdings (6,845 billion yen) to operating asset value, and subtracting out debt (11,862 billion yen) and minority interests (583 billion yen) from this number, yields a value of equity. Dividing this value by the number of shares outstanding (3,448 million) yields a value per share of 4,735 yen, well above the market price of 3,060 yen per share at the time.

$$\frac{19,640 + 2,288 + 6,845 - 11,862 - 583}{3.448} = 4,735 \text{ yen/share}$$

With commodity companies, the variable that causes the volatility is the price of the commodity. Consequently, normalization with commodity companies has to be built around a normalized commodity price.

VALUE DRIVER #1: NORMALIZED EARNINGS

A cyclical firm should be valued based upon earnings in a normal economic year, not earnings at the peak or trough of a cycle. Looking past the ups and downs of economic cycles, what are the normalized earnings for your company?

What is a normalized price for oil? Or gold? There are two ways of answering this question. One is to look at the average price of the commodity over time, adjusted for inflation. The other is to determine a fair price for the commodity, given the demand and supply for that commodity. Once you have normalized the price of the commodity, you can assess what the revenues, earnings, and cash flows would have been for the company being valued at that normalized price. With revenues and earnings, this may just require multiplying the number of units sold at the normalized price and making reasonable assumptions about costs. With reinvestment and cost of financing, it will require some subjective judgments on how much (if any) the reinvestment and cost of funding numbers would have changed at the normalized price.

Using a normalized commodity price to value a commodity company does expose you to the critique that the valuations you obtain will reflect your commodity price views as much as they do your views of the company. If you want to remove your views of commodity prices from valuations of commodity companies, the safest way to do this is to use market-based prices for the commodity in your forecasts. Since most commodities have forward and futures markets, you can use the prices for these markets to estimate cash flows in the next few years. The advantage of this approach is that it comes with a built-in mechanism for hedging against commodity price risk. An investor who believes that a company is under-valued but is shaky on what will happen to commodity prices in the future can buy stock in the company and sell oil price futures to protect against adverse price movements.

Exxon Mobil (XOM), the largest oil company in the world, reported operating income in excess of $60 billion in 2008, reflecting oil prices that exceeded $100 a barrel early in the year. By early 2009, however, oil prices had dropped to $45 a barrel and the stock was trading at $64.83. If that lower oil price had prevailed over the entire 12-month period, Exxon would have reported only $34.6 billion in operating income. Valuing Exxon with this updated operating income would have generated a value per share of $69.43, suggesting that the stock was mildly undervalued. The approach is flexible enough to reflect a point of view on oil prices. Thus, if you expect oil prices to rise, the value per share for Exxon Mobil will go up. In Figure 10.1, the value of Exxon Mobil is shown as a function of the normalized oil price.

If the normalized oil price is $42.52, the value per share is $64.83, equal to the prevailing stock price. Put

Figure 10.1   Normalized Oil Price and Value per Share for Exxon Mobil

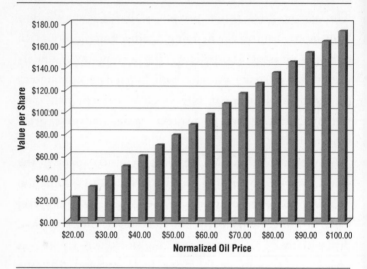

VALUE DRIVER #2: NORMAL COMMODITY PRICES

As commodity prices swing, so will the earnings of a commodity company. For your commodity company, what is a normalized price for the commodity in question, and what is the firm's value at that price?

another way, any investor who believes that the oil price will stabilize above this level will find Exxon Mobil to be undervalued.

Relative Valuation

The two basic approaches that we developed in the discounted cash flow approach—using normalized earnings or adapting the growth rate—are also the approaches we have for making relative valuation work with cyclical and commodity companies.

If the normalized earnings for a cyclical or commodity firm reflect what it can make in a normal year, there has to be consistency in the way the market values companies relative to these normalized earnings. In the extreme case, where there are no growth and risk differences across firms, the PE ratios for these firms, with normalized earnings per share, should be identical across firms. In the more general case, where growth and risk differences persist even after normalization, we would expect to see differences in the multiples that companies trade at. In particular, expect to see firms that have more risky earnings trade at lower multiples of normalized earnings than firms with more stable earnings. We would also expect to see firms that have higher growth potential trade at higher multiples of normalized earnings than firms with lower growth potential. To provide a concrete illustration, Petrobras (PBR) and Exxon Mobil are both oil companies whose earnings are affected by the price of oil. Even if we normalize earnings, thus controlling for the price of oil, Petrobras should trade at a different multiple of earnings than Exxon Mobil, because its earnings are riskier (since they are derived almost entirely from Brazilian reserves) and also because it has higher growth potential.

If you are reluctant to replace the current operating numbers of a company with normalized values, the multiples at which cyclical and commodity firms trade at will change as they move through the cycle. In particular, the multiples of earnings for cyclical and commodity firms will bottom out at the peak of the cycle and be highest at the bottom of the cycle. If the earnings of all companies in a sector move in lock step, there are no serious consequences to comparing the multiples of current earnings that firms trade at. In effect, we may conclude that a steel company with a PE ratio of six is fairly valued at the peak of the cycle, when steel companies collectively report high earnings (and low PE). The same firm may be fairly valued at 15 times earnings at an economic trough, where the earnings of other steel companies are also down.

Table 10.1 reports on PE ratios for oil companies, using earnings per share in the most recent fiscal year, earnings per share in the last four quarters, earnings per share in the next four quarters, and the average earnings per share over the last five years.

With outliers in the data, the sector medians are much more meaningful numbers than the sector averages. There are oil companies that look cheap on one measure

Table 10.1 PE Ratios for Oil Companies in Early 2009

Company Name	Current PE	Trailing PE	Forward PE	Normalized PE
BP PLC ADR	9.69	4.55	8.76	6.00
Chevron Corp.	11.68	5.25	15.31	8.39
ConocoPhillips	7.95	3.55	8.00	6.08
Exxon Mobil Corp.	12.77	7.59	13.15	10.12
Frontier Oil	66.52	18.14	10.35	7.35
Hess Corp.	136.12	7.90	54.45	16.81
Holly Corp.	7.20	9.14	8.01	6.29
Marathon Oil Corp.	11.07	4.57	7.79	5.38
Murphy Oil Corp.	14.24	4.7	14.39	7.45
Occidental Petroleum	17.48	6.2	18.23	10.11
Petroleo Brasileiro ADR	7.52	6.86	7.52	7.34
Repsol-YPF ADR	10.65	4.52	6.43	4.26
Royal Dutch Shell "A"	7.99	4.27	8.49	6.77
Sunoco Inc.	4.99	3.79	7.76	6.59
Tesoro Corp.	5.26	7.77	6.51	4.88
Total ADR	8.54	5.44	8.82	6.97
Average	21.23	6.52	12.75	7.55
Median	10.17	5.35	8.63	6.87

and expensive on the others. Marathon Oil (MRO), for instance, looks overvalued on a current PE basis but undervalued using other earnings measures. Exxon looks overvalued on every earnings measure, whereas Sunoco (SUN) looks undervalued on every one.

The Real Option Argument for Undeveloped Reserves

One critique of conventional valuation approaches is that they fail to consider adequately the interrelationship between the commodity price and the investment and financing actions of commodity companies. In other words, oil companies produce more oil and have more cash to return to stockholders when oil prices are high than they do when oil prices are low. Thus, these firms have options to develop their oil reserves, which they can exercise after observing the oil price, and these options can add to value.

Even if you never explicitly use option-pricing models to value natural resource reserves or firms, there are implications for value.

- *Price volatility affects value:* The value of a commodity company is a function of not only the price of the commodity but also the expected volatility in that price. The price matters for obvious reasons—higher commodity prices translate into higher revenues, earnings, and cash flows. More volatile commodity prices can make undeveloped reserves more valuable.

- *Mature versus growth commodity companies:* As commodity prices become more volatile, commodity companies that derive more of their value from undeveloped reserves will gain in value, relative to more mature companies that generate cash flows from developed reserves. If the oil price volatility is perceived to have increased even though the price itself has not changed, you would expect Petrobras to gain in value relative to Exxon Mobil.

- *Development of reserves:* As commodity price volatility increases, commodity companies will become more reluctant to develop their reserves, holding out for even higher prices.
- *Optionality increases as commodity price decreases:* The option value of reserves is greatest when commodity prices are low (and the reserves are either marginally viable or not viable) and should decrease as commodity prices increase.

If you regard undeveloped reserves as options, discounted cash flow valuation will generally underestimate the value of natural resource companies, because the expected price of the commodity is used to estimate revenues and operating profits. Again, the difference will be greatest for firms with significant undeveloped reserves and with commodities where price volatility is highest.

Value Plays

When investing in a commodity company, you are also investing in the underlying commodity. There are two ways you can incorporate this reality into

(Continued)

your investing strategy. In the first, you take a stand on commodity prices and invest in companies that will benefit the most from your forecasted price move. Thus, if commodity prices are low, and you believe that they will increase significantly in the future, the value payoff will be highest in companies with significant undeveloped reserves of the commodity and the funding to survive near-term adverse price movements. In the second, you accept that you are not a good prognosticator of commodity prices, and focus on picking the best companies in the sector. Look for companies that have significant low-cost reserves and are efficient in finding and exploiting new reserves. To protect yourself against commodity price movements in the future, use commodity futures and options to at least partially hedge your investment in the company.

There are also two analogous investment strategies you can adopt with cyclical companies. The first is to put your faith in your forecasts of overall economic growth. If you believe that overall economic growth will be stronger than the rest of the market thinks it will be, you should buy strong cyclical companies that will benefit from the economic upswing. This strategy is most likely to work in periods of economic malaise, where investors are overreacting to current economic indicators and selling cyclical stocks. The second is a more standard valuation strategy, where you own up to your inability to forecast economic cycles and focus on buying the best bargains in each cyclical sector. In particular, you want to find companies that trade at the same multiple of normalized earnings as the rest of the companies in the sector, while generating higher profit margins and returns on capital on a normalized basis.

The bottom line: No matter how carefully you do your homework, commodity and cyclical companies will see ups and downs in both earnings and prices, as a function of economic and commodity cycles. Ironically, your biggest money-making opportunities come from these cyclical movements.

Chapter Eleven

Invisible Value

~

*Valuing Companies with
Intangible Assets*

IN THE EARLY PART OF THE LAST CENTURY, it was the railroads and manufacturing companies that were the vanguards of the stock market, deriving their power from physical assets—land, factories, and equipment. The most successful companies of our generation have been technology and service companies, with much of their value coming from assets that have no physical presence such as brand name, technological skills, and human capital.

When valuing firms with these intangible assets, investors have to navigate their way through accounting conventions that have not always been consistent with those used for manufacturing firms.

Looking at publicly traded firms, it is obvious that many firms derive the bulk of their value from intangible assets. From consumer product companies, dependent upon brand names, to pharmaceutical companies, with blockbuster drugs protected by patent, to technology companies that draw on their skilled technicians and know-how, these firms range the spectrum. The simplest measure of how much of the economy is represented by intangible assets comes from the market values of firms that derive the bulk of their value from these assets as a proportion of the overall market. While technology firms have fallen back from their peak numbers in 2000, they still represented 14 percent of the overall S&P 500 index at the end of 2008. If we add pharmaceutical and

VALUE DRIVER #1: INTANGIBLE ASSETS

Intangible assets can be human capital, technological prowess, brand name, or a loyal workforce. What are your firm's intangible assets and how did it acquire them?

consumer product companies to this mix, the proportion becomes even higher.

While firms with intangible assets are diverse, there are two characteristics that they do have in common. The first is that the accounting for intangible assets is not consistent with its treatment of physical assets. Accounting first principles suggest a simple rule to separate capital expenses from operating expenses. Any expense that creates benefits over many years is a capital expense, whereas expenses that generate benefits only in the current year are operating expenses. Accountants stay true to this distinction with manufacturing firms, putting investments in plant, equipment, and buildings in the capital expense column, and labor and raw material expenses in the operating expense column. However, they seem to ignore these first principles when it comes to firms with intangible assets. The most significant capital expenditures made by technology and pharmaceutical firms is in R&D, by consumer product companies in brand name advertising, and by consulting firms in training and recruiting personnel. Using the argument that the benefits are too uncertain, accountants have treated these expenses as operating expenses. As a consequence, earnings and capital expenditures tend to be understated at these firms.

The other is that firms with intangible assets are bigger users of options to compensate management than firms in other businesses. Some of this behavior can be attributed to where these firms are in the life cycle (closer to growth than mature), but some of it has to be related to how dependent these firms are on retaining human capital.

Valuation Issues

The miscategorization of capital expenses, the sparing use of debt and the dependence on equity-based compensation (options and restricted stock), can create problems when we value these firms. Put more bluntly, the accounting measures of book value, earnings, and capital expenditures for firms with intangible assets are all misleading, insofar as they do not measure what they claim to measure and because they are not directly comparable to the same items at a manufacturing firm. To value companies with intangible assets, we have to begin by correcting the erroneous accounting classification of capital expenses, and restate the fundamental inputs into value—operating income, capital expenditure, and return on capital. Once we make those corrections, these companies look very much like the companies in other sectors and can be valued using the same metrics.

The same problems play out in relative valuation. The accounting inconsistencies that skew earnings and book value measures in intrinsic valuation models also make it difficult to make comparisons of multiples based upon these values. The PE ratio for a technology company is not directly comparable to the PE ratio for a manufacturing firm, since earnings are not measured consistently across firms. Even within technology firms, it is not clear that a company that trades at a lower multiple of earnings or book value is cheaper than one that trades at a higher multiple.

Valuation Solutions

To value firms with intangible assets, we have to deal with the two big problems that they share. First, we have to clean up the financial statements (income statement and balance sheet) and recategorize operating and capital expenses. The intent is not just to get a better measure of earnings, though that is a side benefit, but also to get a clearer sense of what the firm is investing to generate future growth. Second, we also have to deal more effectively with management options—the ones that have been granted in the past as well the ones that we expect to be granted in the future.

Regaining Accounting Consistency

Using the rationale that the products of research are too uncertain and difficult to quantify, accounting standards have generally required that all R&D expenditure be shown as an operating expense in the period in which it occurs. This has several consequences, but one of the most profound is that the value of the assets created by research does not show up on the balance sheet as part of the total assets of the firm. This, in turn, creates ripple effects for the measurement of capital and profitability ratios for the firm.

Research expenses, notwithstanding the uncertainty about future benefits, should be capitalized. To illustrate the process, we will use Amgen (AMGN), a large biotechnology company. To capitalize and value research assets, we have to make an assumption about how long it takes for research and development to be converted, on average, into commercial products. This is called the *amortizable life* of these assets. This life will vary across firms and reflect the commercial life of the products that emerge from the research. Since the approval process for new drugs is long drawn out, we will use a 10-year amortizable life for Amgen.

Once the amortizable life of research and development expenses has been estimated, the next step is to collect data on R&D expenses over past years ranging back to the amortizable life of the research asset. Thus, if the research asset has an amortizable life of 10 years, as is the case with Amgen, the R&D expenses in each of the 10 years prior to the current one are shown in Table 11.1. (Year –1 is one year ago, –2 is two years ago, and so on.)

For simplicity, it can be assumed that the amortization is uniform over time, and in the case of the research asset

Table 11.1   R&D Amortization for Amgen in early 2009

Year	R&D Expense	Unamortized Portion		Amortization This Year
Current	3030.00	1.00	3030.00	
−1	3266.00	0.90	2939.40	$326.60
−2	3366.00	0.80	2692.80	$336.60
−3	2314.00	0.70	1619.80	$231.40
−4	2028.00	0.60	1216.80	$202.80
−5	1655.00	0.50	827.50	$165.50
−6	1117.00	0.40	446.80	$111.70
−7	864.00	0.30	259.20	$86.40
−8	845.00	0.20	169.00	$84.50
−9	823.00	0.10	82.30	$82.30
−10	663.00	0.00	0.00	$66.30
			$13,283.60	$1,694.10

with a 10-year life, you assume that one-tenth of the expense is written off each year to get the cumulated amortization expense for the current year of $1,604 billion. Adding up the unamortized portion of the expenses from prior years yields the capital invested in the research asset of $13,284 million. This augments the value of the assets of the firm, and by extension, the book value of equity (and capital). For Amgen:

Adjusted book value of equity = Stated book value of equity
+ Capital invested in R&D = $17,869 million
+ $13,284 million = $31,153 million

The reported accounting income is adjusted to reflect the capitalization of R&D expenses. First, the R&D

expenses that were subtracted out to arrive at the operating income are added back to the operating income, reflecting their recategorization as capital expenses. Next, the amortization of the research asset is treated like depreciation is and netted out to arrive at the adjusted operating income and adjusted net income. Using Amgen to illustrate this process:

$$\text{Adjusted operating income} = \text{Stated operating income}$$
$$+ \text{R\&D expenses} - \text{R\&D amortization} = 5,594$$
$$+ 3,030 - 1,694 = \$6.930 \text{ million}$$

$$\text{Adjusted net income} = \text{Net income} + \text{R\&D expenses}$$
$$- \text{R\&D Amortization} = 4,196 + 3,030$$
$$- 1,694 = \$5,532 \text{ million}$$

The adjusted operating income will generally increase for firms that have R&D expenses that are growing over time.

For Amgen, using the augmented book values of equity and capital, with the adjusted income, yields very different estimates for return measures in Table 11.2.

While the profitability ratios for Amgen remain impressive even after the adjustment, they decline significantly from the unadjusted numbers.

While R&D expenses are the most prominent example of capital expenses being treated as operating expenses, there are other operating expenses that arguably should be

Table 11.2   Effects of Capitalizing Research Expenses for Amgen

	Unadjusted	Adjusted for R&D
Return on equity	$\dfrac{4{,}196}{17{,}869} = 23.48\%$	$\dfrac{5{,}532}{(17{,}869 + 13{,}284)} = 17.75\%$
Pre-tax return on capital	$\dfrac{5{,}594}{21{,}985} = 25.44\%$	$\dfrac{6{,}930}{(21{,}985 + 13{,}284)} = 19.65\%$

treated as capital expenses. Consumer product companies such as Procter & Gamble (PG) and Coca Cola (KO) could make a case that a portion of advertising expenses should be treated as capital expenses, since they are designed to augment brand name value. For a consulting firm like KPMG or McKinsey, the cost of recruiting and training its employees could be considered a capital expense, since the consultants who emerge are likely to be the heart of the firm's value and provide benefits over many years. For many new technology firms, including online retailers such as Amazon.com, the biggest operating expense item is selling, general, and administrative expenses (SG&A). These firms could argue that a portion of these expenses should be treated as capital expenses since they are designed to increase brand name awareness and bring in new, presumably long term, customers.

While these arguments have some merit, we remain wary about using them to justify capitalizing these expenses. For an operating expense to be capitalized there should be substantial evidence that the benefits from the expense accrue over multiple periods. Does a customer who is enticed to buy from Amazon (AMZN), based upon an advertisement or promotion, continue as a customer for the long term? There are some analysts who claim that this is indeed the case and attribute significant value added to each new customer. It would be logical, under those circumstances, to capitalize these expenses using a procedure similar to that used to capitalize R&D expenses.

1. Determine the period over which the benefits from the operating expense (such as SG&A) will flow.
2. Estimate the value of the asset (similar to the research asset) created by these expenses. This amount will be added to the book value of equity/capital and used to estimate the returns on equity and capital.
3. Adjust the operating income for the expense and the amortization of the created asset.

VALUE DRIVER #2: EFFICIENCY OF INTANGIBLE INVESTMENTS

Not all investments in intangible assets create value. In your firm, how quickly do investments in intangible assets pay off as profits? How much does the firm earn from these investments and for how long?

The net effects of the capitalization will be seen most visibly in the reinvestment rates and returns on capital you estimate for these firms.

Intrinsic Valuation

When you capitalize the expenses associated with creating intangible assets, you are in effect redoing the financial statements of the firm and restating numbers that are fundamental inputs into valuation—earnings, reinvestment, and measures of returns.

Earnings: Adding back the current year's expense and subtracting out the amortization of past expenses, the effect on earnings will generally be positive if expenses have risen over time. With Amgen, for instance, where R&D expenses increased from $663 million at the start of the amortization period to $3.03 billion in the current year, the earnings increased by more than $1.3 billion as a result of the R&D adjustment.

Reinvestment: The effect on reinvestment is identical to the effect on earnings, with reinvestment increasing or decreasing by exactly the same amount as earnings. That will generally increase the reinvestment rate.

Capital invested: Since the unamortized portion of the prior year's expenses is treated as an asset, it adds to the estimated equity or capital invested in the firm. The effect will increase with the amortizable life and should therefore be higher for pharmaceutical firms (where amortizable lives tend to be longer) than for software firms (where research pays off far more quickly as commercial products).

Return on equity (capital): Since both earnings and capital invested are affected by capitalization, the net effects on return on equity and capital are unpredictable. If the return on equity (capital) increases after the recapitalization, it can be considered a rough indicator that the returns earned by the firm on its R&D is greater than its returns on traditional investments.

In addition to providing us with more realistic estimates of what these firms are investing in their growth and the quality of their investments, the capitalization process also restores consistency to valuations by ensuring that growth rates are in line with reinvestment and return on capital assumptions. Thus, technology or pharmaceutical firms that want to continue to grow have to keep investing in R&D, while ensuring that these investments, at least collectively, generate high returns for the firm.

How much of an impact will capitalizing R&D have on the value per share? To illustrate, we valued Amgen,

Table 11.3   Valuation Fundamentals: With and Without R&D Capitalization

	Conventional	Capitalized R&D
After-tax ROC	14.91%	17.41%
Reinvestment rate	19.79%	33.23%
Growth rate	2.95%	5.78%
Value per share	$43.63	$62.97

using both the unadjusted accounting numbers and the numbers adjusted for capitalized R&D. The numbers are summarized in Table 11.3.

The value per share would have been $43.63 if we had used conventional accounting numbers, about 10 percent under the stock price at the time of $47.97. With capitalized R&D, the value per share is significantly higher and the stock looks cheap. In general, the effect on value will be negative for firms that invest large amounts in R&D, with little to show (yet) in terms of earnings and cash flows in subsequent periods. It will be positive for firms that reinvest large amounts in R&D and report large increases in earnings in subsequent periods. In the case of Amgen, capitalizing R&D has a positive effect on value per share, because of its track record of successful R&D.

Relative Valuation

It is true that all technology and pharmaceutical companies operate under the same flawed accounting rules, expensing R&D rather than capitalizing it. That does not mean, though, that there are no consequences for relative valuation. The effect of capitalizing R&D on earnings and book value can vary widely across firms and will depend upon the following:

- *Age of the firm and stage in life cycle:* Generally speaking, the proportional effects of capitalization on earnings and book value will be much greater at young growth firms than at more mature firms.
- *Amortizable life:* The effect of capitalizing expenses will be much greater as we extend the amortizable life of R&D, especially on capital invested. If different firms within the same business convert research into commercial products at different speeds, the effect on earnings of capitalizing R&D can vary across firms.

If you ignore accounting inconsistencies and use the reported earnings and book values of firms in the computation of multiples, younger firms or firms that have R&D with longer gestation periods will look overvalued (even if they are fairly priced or bargains). Their earnings and book value will be understated, leading to much higher PE, EV/EBITDA, and book value multiples for these firms.

There are two ways to incorporate these factors into relative valuation. The first is to capitalize the expenses associated with investing in intangible assets for each firm and to compute consistent measures of earnings and book value to use in multiples. This approach, while yielding the most precision, is also the most time and data intensive. The second is to stick with the reported accounting values for earnings and book value, while controlling for the factors listed above.

Table 11.4 presents a relative valuation of pharmaceutical firms, using three measures of PE ratios: the conventional PE ratio (obtained by dividing the market capitalization by the net income); a measure of PE computed using the sum of net income and R&D; and an adjusted measure, where you net out the amortization of R&D (Net income + R&D expense − Amortization of R&D).

Astra Zeneca (AZN) looks undervalued, using every measure of PE and Celgene (CELG) looks overvalued on all three measures. Bristol Myers (BMY) looks overvalued on a conventional PE ratio, slightly undervalued on the augmented earnings measure, and correctly valued on the net R&D measure. We would argue that the last measure, with both R&D and its amortization incorporated yields the fairest comparison.

Table 11.4 Price/Earnings Ratios: Pharmaceutical Companies

Company Name	PE	P/(E + R&D)	P/(E + Net R&D)
Abbott Labs.	14.62	9.43	13.91
Allergan Inc.	18.89	7.93	13.10
Astra Zeneca PLC	7.24	3.92	6.54
Biogen Idec Inc.	16.26	6.86	10.63
Bristol-Myers Squibb	16.18	6.09	12.18
Celgene Corp.	80.84	29.26	41.46
Genzyme Corp.	34.08	8.30	13.76
Gilead Sciences	20.04	14.75	16.89
GlaxoSmithKline ADR	7.31	4.48	7.16
Lilly (Eli)	8.08	4.05	7.31
Merck & Co.	5.98	3.70	5.76
Novartis AG ADR	9.79	8.00	9.70
Novo Nordisk ADR	16.76	9.24	13.83
Pfizer Inc.	10.54	5.32	9.87
Sanofi-Aventis	9.61	5.83	9.03
Schering-Plough	13.91	9.62	12.99
Teva Pharmaceutical	14.44	10.85	13.21
Wyeth	12.31	6.98	11.90
Average	**17.61**	**8.59**	**12.74**
Median	**14.18**	**7.46**	**12.04**

Dealing with Equity Options

Firms that pay managers and others with equity options are giving away some of the stockholders' equity to these people. To deal with the resulting loss in value to common stockholders, there are three approaches that are employed in intrinsic valuation, and we will use Google (GOOG), in early 2009, to illustrate all three. In February 2009, we estimated a value for equity in the aggregate of $102,345 million for Google; the firm had 315.29 million shares outstanding and 13.97 million in options outstanding, with an average strike price of $391.40/share.

1. Assume that all or some of the options will be exercised in the future, adjust the number of shares outstanding and divide the value of equity by this number to arrive at value per share; this is the diluted shares approach. To estimate the value of equity per share in Google, divide the aggregate value of equity estimated by the total number of shares outstanding, including options.

$$\frac{\text{Aggregate Value of Equity}}{\text{Fully diluted number of shares}} = \frac{102,345}{(315.29 + 13.97)} = \$310.83\,/\,\text{share}$$

While this approach has the virtue of simplicity, it will lead to too low an estimate of value per share, because it fails to reflect the proceeds from option exercise. In Google's case, each option that is exercised will bring in cash to the firm.

2. Incorporate the exercise proceeds from the options in the numerator and then divide by the number of shares that would be outstanding after exercise;

this is the treasury stock approach. Using this stock approach on Google:

$$\frac{\text{Value of equity} + \text{Options outstanding} * \text{Average exercise price}}{\text{Fully diluted number of shares}}$$

$$= \frac{\$102,345 + 13.97 * \$391.40}{(315.29 + 13.97)} = \$327.44/\text{share}$$

This approach will yield too high a value per share, largely because the approach ignores the time premium on the option; an option trading at or out of the money may have no exercise value but it still has option value.

3. Estimate the value of the options today, given today's value per share and the time premium on the option. Once this value has been estimated, it is subtracted from the estimated equity value, and the remaining amount is divided by the number of shares outstanding to arrive at value per share. Based upon the exercise price ($391.40) and the average maturity (3.50 years), the options outstanding at Google are valued at $897 million and the resulting value per share is $321.76.

$$\frac{\text{Value of equity} - \text{Value of options}}{\text{Primary shares outstanding}} = \frac{102,345 - 897}{315.29} = \$321.76$$

When choosing which approach to take, consider that the first is the crudest, the second is slightly more tempered, and the third is the most work, but it is the right way to deal with options. The fact that most investors and analysts do not go to the trouble may provide an opportunity for those who go the extra mile in assessing options.

Comparing multiples across companies is complicated by the fact that firms often have varying numbers of employee options outstanding and these options can have very different values. A failure to explicitly factor these options into analysis will result in companies with unusually large or small (relative to the peer group) numbers of options outstanding looking misvalued on a relative basis. With PE ratios, for instance, using primary earnings per share will make companies with more options outstanding look cheap. Using fully diluted earnings per share will make firms that have long-term, deep in-the-money options outstanding look cheap. The only way to incorporate the effect of options into earnings multiples is to value the options at fair value, using the current stock price as the basis, and add this value on to the market capitalization to arrive at the total market value of equity.

Table 11.5 summarizes a comparison of Google and Cisco (CSCO) on a PE ratio basis, with different approaches for dealing with options. While Cisco looks cheaper than Google, using all three measures of PE ratios, it looks cheapest on a primary PE ratio basis and less so with an option value approach.

Table 11.5   Option Adjusted PE Ratios for Google and Cisco

	Google	Cisco
Stock price	$326.60	$16.23
Primary PE	24.37	11.04
Diluted PE	25.45	13.25
Market capitalization	$102,975	$97,153
Value of options	$1,406	$3,477
Market capitalization + Value of options	$104,381	$100,630
Net Income before option expensing	$5,347	$8,802
Net Income after option expensing	$4,227	$8,052
Adjusted PE	24.69	12.50

Value Plays

The biggest hurdle when investing in firms with intangible assets is that the accounting numbers, at least as stated, are deceptive. As an investor, you have to correct for these accounting problems and focus on companies that have the following characteristics:

- *Intangible assets that generate high returns:* For intangible assets to generate value, they have to earn high returns. Look for a firm with intangible assets that are unique and difficult to replicate.
- *Reasonable prices for "true" earnings:* Many firms with intangible assets have high growth potential and are priced to reflect that growth. Using the mismatch test, invest in companies that have high

growth in earnings, corrected for accounting miscategorization, and that trade at low multiples of these corrected earnings.

- *Spending to preserve and augment these intangible assets:* Intangible assets do not always stay valuable, especially if they are ignored. Focus on firms that invest in these assets (by spending on R&D, recruiting, or advertising) to preserve and grow value.

- *Spending is efficient:* Not all expenditures on intangible assets generate value. Keep tabs on investments in intangible assets to see how quickly and how well they pay off and steer your money towards firms that rank highly on both dimensions.

- *Equity claims drain per share value:* Firms with intangible assets tend to be big users of equity options as compensation, which can affect equity value per share. Incorporate the effects of outstanding options into your estimates of value per share and avoid companies that are cavalier about issuing new options to managers.

In effect, you want to invest in companies that make investments in intangible assets and are able to leverage these assets to generate high returns, while protecting your share of equity ownership.

Conclusion

————— ∾ —————

Rules for the Road

THE MORE THINGS CHANGE, THE MORE THEY STAY THE same. As we employed both intrinsic and relative valuation techniques to value firms across the life cycle from Evergreen Solar, a young growth company, to Sears, a company whose best days are behind it, we followed a familiar script. The enduring theme is that value rests on standard ingredients: cash flows, growth, and risk, though the effects of each can vary across companies and across time.

Common Ingredients

No matter what type of company you are valuing, you have to decide whether you are valuing just equity or the entire business, the approach you will use to estimate value (intrinsic versus relative valuation), and the key components of value.

When valuing a business, you can choose to value the equity in the business or you can value the entire business. If you value the business, you can get to the value of equity by adding back assets that you have not valued yet (cash and cross holdings) and subtracting out what you owe (debt). The choice matters because all of your inputs—cash flows, growth, and risk—have to be defined consistently. For most of the companies that we have valued in this book, we have valued the businesses and backed into the value of equity. With financial service firms, our inability to define debt and estimate cash flows did push us into using equity valuation models.

You can also value a business based on its fundamentals, which is the intrinsic value, or you can value it by looking at how the market prices similar firms in the market. While both approaches yield estimates of value, they answer different questions. With intrinsic valuation, the question we are answering is: Given this company's cash flows and risk, it is under- or overvalued? With relative valuation, the question being answered is: Is this company cheap or expensive, given how the market is pricing other companies just like this one? With the example of Under Armour in Chapter 6, the intrinsic valuation approach led us to conclude that the company was undervalued, whereas the relative valuation would have led us to conclude that the stock is overvalued.

In both intrinsic and relative valuation, the value of a company rests on three ingredients: cash flows from existing assets, the expected growth in these cash flows, and the discount rate that reflects the risk in those cash flows. In intrinsic valuation, we are explicit about our estimates for these inputs. In relative valuation, we try to control for differences across firms on these inputs, when comparing how they are priced.

Differences in Emphasis

The models and approaches used are identical for all companies, but the choices we make and the emphasis we put on inputs varied across companies. As illustrated in Table 12.1, the value drivers that were highlighted in each chapter reflect the shifts in focus, as firms move through the life cycle and across sectors.

These value drivers are useful not only to investors who want to determine what companies offer the best investment odds, but also to managers in these firms, in terms of where they should be focusing their attention to increase value.

And the Payoff

Can you make money on your valuations? The answer depends on three variables. The first is the quality of your valuation.

Table 12.1   Value Drivers across the Life Cycle and Sectors

Category	Value Drivers
Young growth companies	Revenue growth, target margin, survival probability
Growth companies	Scaling growth, margin sustainability
Mature companies	Operating slack, financial slack, probability of management change
Declining companies	Going concern value, default probability, default consequences
Financial service firms	Equity risk, quality of growth (return on equity), regulatory capital buffers
Commodity and cyclical companies	Normalized earnings, excess returns, Long-term growth
Intangible asset companies	Nature of intangible assets, efficiency of investments in intangible assets

Well done valuations based upon better information should generate better returns than shoddy valuations based upon rumor or worse. The second is market feedback. To make money on even the best-done valuation, the market has to correct its mistakes. The payoff to valuation is likely to be speedier and more lucrative in smoothly functioning markets. In more selfish terms, you want the market to be efficient for the most part, with pockets of inefficiency that you can exploit. The third and final factor is luck. While this will violate your sense of fairness, luck can overwhelm good valuation skills. While you cannot depend on good luck, you can reduce the impact of luck on your returns by spreading your bets across many companies that you have found to be undervalued. Diversification still pays!

Parting Words

Do not let experts and investment professionals intimidate you. All too often, they are using the same information that you are and their understanding of valuation is no deeper than yours. Do not be afraid to make mistakes. I hope that even if not all of your investments are winners, the process of analyzing investments and assessing value brings you as much joy as it has brought me.

---

10 Rules for the Road

1. Feel free to abandon models, but do not budge on first principles.
2. Pay heed to markets, but do not let them determine what you do.
3. Risk affects value.
4. Growth is not free and is not always good for value.
5. All good things, including growth, come to an end. Nothing is forever.

(*Continued*)

---

6. Watch out for truncation risk; many firms do not make it.
7. Look at the past, but think about the future.
8. Remember the law of large numbers. An average is better than a single number.
9. Accept uncertainty, face up to it and deal with it.
10. Convert stories to numbers.